THE CROSS
AND
THE DRAGON

Donald H. Kauffman

Little
Ones †

LITTLE ONES BOOKS
Young America, Minnesota, U.S.A.
and Toronto, Ontario, Canada

ISBN-0-920195-02-4

Published by LITTLE ONES BOOKS'
Young America, Minnesota, U.S.A.
and Toronto, Ontario, Canada
123 Eastside Drive

Printed by HARMONY PRINTING LIMITED
123 Eastside Drive, Toronto, Ontario, Canada

Foreword

When Don Kauffman, a highly respected servant of the Lord, asked me to read the manuscript of **The Cross and the Dragon**, I was immediately interested because of the information I had received over the years of his missionary parents.

From the opening paragraph of the first chapter entitled, "The Dragon," one is informed of the history of the great people of China who are very intelligent, warm, loving and who possess a long and rich history and culture. When one learns of the true dominant religions of that nation, one begins to understand why this country is so complex.

The historical background and account of the great Protestant missionary movement which had its beginning at the start of the 19th century tells how the Dragon was challenged. The enormity of the task of trying to penetrate a land where the people were too humanistic, too pessimistic and too fatalistic was summarized best by Dr. Nelson Bell (Dr. Billy Graham's father-in-law), a former medical missionary to China, where he said, "Nor can I imagine greater conceit than to imagine that one by one's own force of personality and attractiveness, could win one soul to Christ. God uses the witness of the Chirst-like life, and there is not a missionary in China who is not praying and daily striving, by God's grace, to so live and act that He may be glorified."

When I read the account of the knight – Ivan Kauffman – the dragon fighter's conversion, his call, and his response to his mission to take the gospel to the forbidden land of Tibet, I was tremendously moved in my spirit.

The spiritual warfare, the personal sacrifice, the dauntless courage, the triumphant faith and the success of the gospel is a story that evoked a response in my own life as to my commitment to the gospel.

This book should be required reading for all Christians and certainly any candidate who senses the call to full-time ministry.

I believe this book could change the attitude of Christian young people and turn them into an army of volunteers who will not ask what the gospel can do for them, but rather, what they can do for the gospel.

This book has powerfully impacted my life. My prayer is that it will do the same for you.

Rev. James MacKnight
General Superintendent
Pentecostal Assemblies of Canada

"This book is dedicated to my wife, Irene, and our sons, Dale and Noel, who were raised among the Chinese people, a great people who have buried 20 dynasties and will also bury this one."

Special thanks to Miss June Deacon for proofreading the manuscript.

Table of Contents

Chapter I

The Dragon

Introducing the Dragon

The dragon has played a great part throughout all Chinese history. The Emperor was closely connected with the dragon god. His throne was called "The Dragon Throne." When war, revolution, flood or famine came, the Chinese felt it was because the priests and Emperor had failed to control the dragons. Then the indignant and ruined peasantry had a right to overthrow the dynasty and start a new line strong enough to control the dragons. Until the days of revolution of 1911, the Chinese flag was a great dragon upon a yellow background. That flag has gone, but the people still believe in the dragon.

This simple, rather superstitious, animistic belief in a great dragon, who was the cause of their misery, was perhaps closer to the truth in explaining what has kept China bound in misery these many centuries than the later humanistic religions that sprang up.

The Word of God describes him thus in Revelation 20:2 as "...the dragon, that old serpent, which is the Devil, and Satan..." Thus, one-fourth of the world's population has suffered under the one whom the Bible describes as a "thief" who comes not but to kill and to destroy. The largely humanistic religions or philosophies have been helpless to set the people free from the tyranny of the dragon. They have, no doubt, been opiates that he has used to try to lull the people to sleep spiritually.

The Three Religions of China

We will not go into any detail concerning the three main religions of China, except to mention them briefly. The three men who founded these religions were Confucius, Sakyamuni (Buddha) and Lao-tze. Of this triumvirate, Lao-tze, though the

1

junior in influence, was the senior in chronology. The three were loosely contemporaries. Lao-tze, a senior contemporary of Confucius, lived in the same age as Buddha in India and Jeremiah and Ezekiel among the prophets of Israel. There is strong evidence that the knowledge of Jehovah God came to China in the early dynasties. For instance, the early Emperors used to offer sacrifices to the Emperor of Heaven on the marble altar of the Temple of Heaven in Peking in atonement for the sins of the people and pray for a good harvest. Also, the pattern of many of the temples in China is much like the Tabernacle pattern given by God to Moses, with a large outer court, a small inner court and, finally, a small inner building (like the "Holy of holies") that houses deity.

"For even though they knew God, they did not honor Him as God, or give thanks; but they became futile in their speculations, and their foolish heart was darkened. Professing to be wise, they became fools, and exchanged the glory of the incorruptible God for an image in the form of corruptible man and of birds and four-footed animals and crawling creatures" (Romans 1:21, 22, 23, NASB).

Confucianism

If we look briefly at these religions, we see that they all have some truth in them but each one lacks something vital. Confucianism is *too humanistic*. There is no concept of a supreme being, and they did not speak of 'Sheung Di' or the Emperor of Heaven. Confucius laid great stress on the value of collective existence and the search for harmonious social and political frameworks within which *ethical behavior*, rather than naked force or personal profit, would prevail. He stressed the value of the family which was extended to include the Emperor, who was the head of the whole human family; and obedience to local and central government officials was expected to be as complete as that to one's own father and grandfather. Within this basically authoritarian society, great importance was attached to the dignity, if not the autonomy, of the individual. This is the root of the institution which westerners tend to find most perplexing — that of 'face.' 'Face' is required in any dealings between two or more people. Proper respect for each person's feelings should be shown. Precisely because the individual had to repress so many of his own desires in order to fit into the Chinese social order, he clings most tenaciously to the psychological umbrella of 'face,' which allows him to maintain his own self-respect, even when he is at the losing end of the encounter.

Lin Yutang, in her book, "My Country, My People," says: "Confucianism omitted from social relationships, man's social obligations toward the stranger, and great and catastrophic was the omission...In the end, as it worked out, the family became a walled castle outside which everything was legitimate loot."[1] No doubt this enabled China to isolate herself from the rest of the world.

Today, in China, communism is being grown on good soil in the sense that individualism has not yet blossomed. It was therefore possible for Lin Piao, the defence minister and Mao's sometime chosen heir, to observe: "Every person is affiliated with a certain class...there is no such thing as abstract or independent individuals."[2]

The traditional Chinese family included all deceased, all present and all prospective members. A person saw himself as only a temporary holder and transmitter of a family heritage much greater in importance than any particular generation, not to mention any particular individual. The family provided the only social services available to the individual: financial security, social position, protection against outsiders, and even the assurance, in old age, of being honored and supported by one's sons. Thus, Confucianism continues to shape the thinking of the Chinese race even today. It was a philosophy without the inner power to enable the adherent to put into practice from the heart its teachings. Some very good teachings echoed the Bible, such as, "What you would not wish done to yourself, never do to others." Confucius, as Dennis Bloodworth neatly observes, wanted gentlemen but produced *players* instead.[1a]

While Confucianism has given to China a series of excellent lectures on the subject, "Thou shalt love thy neighbor as thyself," the Chinese will have to go to the Gospel of Christ for the yet more fundamental underlying law of life that alone will give credence to the former, "Thou shalt love the Lord thy God with all thy heart, and with all thy soul, and with all thy mind." Only then can one be set free from love of self so as to love one's neighbor as oneself.

Taoism

Taoism, founded by Lao-tze, is *too fantastic*. Although it speaks of a supreme being who is needed in the centre, he remains too much an intangible and incomprehensible

3

abstraction. Lao-tze failed to draw the distinction between man and the matter or objects of nature. Hence, his pantheistic teaching is called the "Law of Nature." Its teachings, in many of the classics, such as "The Book of Rites," seem to us too dream-like and do not face the reality of fallen man. One quotation says, "When the Great Way (Tao) is followed all under heaven will work for the common good. They will choose the virtuous and able. They will advocate sincerity and cultivate peace. Idleness on the part of those who can work will be frowned on. No one will be for himself."[3] Good humanistic ideology. But unless one has a personal relationship with Him who is The Way, The Truth and The Life, it is impossible of fulfillment. The Tao contains much good truth but falls short again of revealing the way to know this great God of the Universe and to know His presence indwelling and changing us. With this kind of idealistic dreaming, no wonder the communists called religion the "opiate of the people."

Buddhism

Buddhism, founded by Guatama Sakyamuni, was imported from India around 58-75 A.D., and is really a foreign religion to China. Buddhism is *too pessimistic* or fatalistic. Buddhism holds out the promise of ultimate personal salvation through escape from the endless cycle of pain. It teaches the life process according to the law of Karma, through transmigration and reincarnation. They had evolution long before Darwin. Not only can the Buddhist exhibit his wisdom by claiming to have come from a monkey, he can, on the other hand, if he so prefers, go back to be a monkey or even a donkey. In fact, he will be one, if he is not careful. As a slave of sin, man is forever chained to the wheel as a debtor of Karma (retribution), and no release can be had until the last farthing is paid. The only escape from this vicious circle is to gain merits from many lifetimes, and one will then be absorbed into Nirvana, a state of non-existence and rest from rebirth. It does not teach of a supreme being, and appeals to the mind of man. Its complicated philosophies are really humanistic, as the deification of man is its ultimate aim. All its gods are men who have died and obtained enlightenment.

The idea is so remote and abstract, and the process involved is so long and difficult that very few people have a heart stout enough even to hope for its achievement. This way of salvation is so difficult and forbidding that Hui-yuan, a Chinese monk who lived in 333-416 A.D., started the Pure Land School. Taking a page from the Bible, he preached the doctrine of "salvation by grace through faith" in the Amitabha Fu (Buddha of Infinite Splendor), through whose grace the believer may be born after death into western paradise. The way to get there is not merely by means of small good works, but by keeping in mind, with thoughts undisturbed, the Amitabha Buddha; constantly relying upon him and calling upon his name. Thus, no prayer is repeated so often by so many people in China as "Nan-Mo O-Mi-T'o Fu," or "I turn to Amitabha Buddha in reverence and trust." Their paradise is a much more attractive place than Nirvana, and resembles somewhat the Bible paradise. There are also many hells, and these are described in very gruesome detail. This sect is known as the lotus sect and has the largest following in China. It is a very tolerant religion, teaching meekness and non-violence, kindness and compassion, charity and almsgiving, reflection and meditation. Thus, a modern effort has been made to make Buddhism less pessimistic. But, at best, it can only administer an injection of anaesthetic to make the suffering of this present life seem less painful.

Many Chinese may claim to be Buddhists but, in truth, they may also be Confucianists and Taoists, as these three religions are so interwoven in the Chinese mind, that to unravel them is well nigh impossible.

The People

Let us make it clear that I am not talking about the Chinese people as such, but about the spiritual forces that have influenced them for centuries. The dragon may have deceived many of the people of China, but they remain precious in God's sight and are China's greatest treasure. If, despite all the stupid cruelties of politics and man-made religion, China still remains a great nation, subtle, and so supremely civilized, it is due to its people. They have buried twenty dynasties, and they will also bury this one. They have not changed. As usual, they are patient; they are not in a hurry. They know so much more than those who rule over them! Someone has described the history of China as in two stages: firstly, the periods when the people manage to enjoy a stable slave condition; and secondly, the periods when the people wish in vain to enjoy a stable slave condition. It is a cycle of chaos and order, order and chaos. Through all the cycles, the ordinary man keeps on working hard and enjoying the simple things of life, such as his family and his food. Chinese cooking, now world-famous, is essentially poor man's food, famine cooking. Its inventive resources were stimulated by the need to use everything, to waste nothing, to salvage the most miserable, least appetizing ingredients which richer nations would reject as waste, and turn them into appetizing food. Fish heads, duck's feet, cow and pig stomachs, snakes, offal, tendons and nerves, dog meat and cat meat become prized delicacies. Thus do the Chinese manage to enrich all the events of life, even the most irksome and barren, and make something savory out of them.

I have seen thin, underfed coolies sweating under heavy loads that a strong man would have strained to lift, let alone carry long distances, squatting or 'hunkering' down in the shade of a tree, laughing and smiling as they enjoy the simple joy of rest. This ability to organize small islands of happiness, even in seas of direct hardship, has always roused the wonderment of the visitor to China.

The Chinese have learned to compartmentalize their lives. They like to keep their beliefs a part of their inner life, while outwardly they seem to flow with the particular ideology that is in power. Thus, when visiting China, most of the people one meets will mouth the Party line; but when you speak to those that have escaped to Hong Kong, you find that they have not really been changed in their inner man by communist ideology. The average Chinese has three basic beliefs. First, he believes in heaven or a supreme being. A lost man is described in Chinese as a man who fears neither heaven nor earth. There is no hope for such a man, they say. Second, they have an unshaken belief that virtue alone will survive. Every Chinese play has a moral, with usually one of four topics: patriotism, filial piety, conjugal faithfulness, or loyalty among friends. Today, modern ideals have muddied these virtues, but they still remain buried deep. Third, they believe that the superior man diligently seeks after truth and righteousness, while the inferior man goes after gain. Thus, the scholar is honored above the merchant in China.

The Chinese people, like the country, can be divided into two main divisions, northern and southern — two distinct types. The northerner is tall, broad-shouldered, slow of speech and slow to anger. The southerner is short, slender and agile, excitable and fiery of temper. In this difference of temperament lies much of Chinese history.

Chapter II

The Dragon Challenged

The Missionary

Into this kingdom of the dragon came the missionary to challenge this too humanistic, too fantastic, too pessimistic, too fatalistic mind-set that had controlled the minds of one-quarter of the world's population — a very intelligent, warm, loving people with a long and rich history and culture. It has become popular to malign the missionary of that day. Such writers as James Mitchner and Pearl Buck (the agnostic daughter of a Southern Presbyterian missionary to China) have pictured them as ignorant, arrogant, superstitious and crude, and state that they should have stayed home rather than try to convert other people of other cultures much older than theirs and perhaps just as rich. The more subtle influences of social Christianity have called for an end to preaching and have urged that the spirit of Christ be manifested solely by mode of life and social assistance. I like the way Dr. Nelson Bell (Dr. Billy Graham's father-in-law), a former medical missionary to China, has answered this. He wrote, in **Christianity Today,**

> It is unthinkable that one should go as a missionary and have in one's heart the knowledge of God, His Son, our Saviour, and the offer of eternal life to all who believe, and then to remain silent. Nor can I imagine greater conceit than to imagine that one, by one's own force of personality and attractiveness, could win one soul to Christ. God uses the witness of the Christ-like life, and there is not a missionary in China who is not praying and daily striving, by God's grace, to so live and act that He may be glorified; but the fact remains that we are told that it is the preaching of the cross, the gospel of redemption from sin through faith in the shed blood of the Saviour which is the 'power of God'.[4]

At the beginning of the 19th century the first Protestant missionary invaded the kingdom of the dragon. Let us examine the historical background of the dragon kingdom at that time.

Historical Background: 1644-1807

In 1644 a few thousand Manchu warriors captured Peking, bringing to an end the reign of the Ming Emperors. The Ch'ing dynasty, which was thus established, endured until the revolution in 1911. During this period, China attained a degree of wealth and power which was not inferior to that of other dynasties: Han, T'ang, Sung Yuan (Mongol) and Ming. By the end of the 18th century, however, the Ch'ing dynasty had passed its greatest period.

It had been a proud dynasty. K'ang Hsi, the greatest Emperor of this dynasty, had invited the Jesuits to China to teach astronomy. But when they began to oppose the traditional religions of China and endeavored to convert the people to the worship of the Emperor of Heaven (Sheung Di), he expelled them from China in 1718. His haughty attitude toward the West is seen in this communique to the court of the western powers: "As your Ambassador can see for himself, we possess all things, I see no value of things strange and ingenious, and have no use for your country's manufactures."[5]

The western powers did not cause China's decay in the 19th century; they simply took advantage of it. The decay was caused by the pressure of population on the land. An extended period of peace brought about a rapid increase in population only to be followed by general chaos as more and more peasants turned to banditry as their only hope of survival. During the century, 1741 to 1841, the population of China, a land approximately the size of the United States, leapt from 140 million to 410 million. Repeated droughts and floods along the banks of its great rivers caused much misery and suffering also.

However, many Chinese do not see the failures of this time as just the result of deficiencies within their own nation or culture or religion, but they attribute them directly to the intervention of foreign powers. Although China has never been colonized as such, through the treaty ports and foreign concessions in these ports, they have been exploited and humbled. Leaders such as Ho Chi Minh, Sun Yat-sen, Chiang Kai-shek and even Mao Tse-tung, were all influenced in their early revolutionary efforts in these enclaves of virtual foreign rule in China.

The newly industrialized western powers began to seek out trade routes to the east and saw in China and its exotic culture and products a chance for wealth and power. Trade with China from the west was hampered, however, until the west found things that China really wanted. China's civilization, because of its geological isolation, was formed in virtual isolation from the west. It is bounded on the east by the vast expanse of the largest ocean in the world, and on the west by the highest mountains in the world and the vast deserts of sand and wasteland. The Chinese, therefore, looked upon themselves as the very center of world civilization. The name they gave their nation, "Jung Kuo," means the "middle kingdom." The Emperor, who stood on the great round marble altar of the "Temple of Heaven" to make his sacrifice and prayer to "Sheung Di," the Emperor of Heaven, believed that he was doing it from the center of the earth. Thus, even today it is difficult for the Chinese leaders to deal with a poly-cultural world of equal sovereign states. They have always looked on the rest of the world as barbarians who could never be their equals in trade or culture.

By the end of the 18th century the west had found products that China wanted. From America, silver and root ginseng and furs were found to be prized by the Chinese. Sandalwood from Hawaii was shipped to China. England had taken cotton cloth to China, and in 1773 began taking on cargoes of opium at Calcutta and trading it in China. By the end of Ch'ien Lung's (K'ang Hsi's grandson) reign, opium had become a universal habit in China.

Hatred of opium and detestation of the foreigner became nearly synonymous, because the opium that enervated the Chinese enriched the foreigners. By 1800, the Imperial Government had outlawed the importation of opium, and even its cultivation. The English East India Company forbade it to be a part of the cargo declared on the manifests of their ships. But this did not stop the opium trade. Because of the 'get-rich-quick' possibilities and the many who were addicted to the drug, bribes and other means were found to get around the law. The failure of China and the English East India Company (who had the monopoly of trade with England), to regulate the opium trade, was the cause of growing hostility between China and the west.

The First Protestant Missionary
It was into this situation that a young Englishman, Robert Morrison, arrived in China by way of New York and Cape Horn, on September 7, 1807, after a journey of more than seven

months from England. This dauntless young Englishman was the first Protestant missionary to enter China. He, at once, embarked on the difficult task of learning the Chinese language. His assistant, Milne, later said, "To learn Chinese required bodies of brass, lungs of steel, heads of oak, hands of spring steel, eyes of eagles, hearts of apostles, memories of angels, and lives of Methuselah."[6] But learn it he did, in spite of an edict by the Imperial Chinese Government which forbade, on pain of death, all Chinese to teach the language to foreigners. The teacher who did venture to instruct Morrison carried poison on his person so as always to be ready to commit suicide, should he be discovered. Morrison's all-consuming purpose, placed in his heart by the Lord, was to translate the Bible into the language of the 400 million Chinese people.

The First Chinese Bible

Although three hundred years after the death of Mohammed (A.D. 635) the Nestorian Christians had translated into Chinese at least part of the New Testament, it was never made available to the public and was later lost. In 1924, the Italian Franciscan, John of Monte Corvino, translated the New Testament and the Psalms, but this Tartar translation of the New Testament does not appear to have been printed, and it too was lost. Many efforts had been made to plant the church of Christ in China, but it seems that not having the Bible in their own vernacular hindered the seed from taking root and growing in that barren rock. At the age of 46, Francis Xavier, the famous Catholic missionary to Japan, forbidden to enter China and confined to a small island near Macao on the Pearl River entrance, looked with dying eyes on the hills of China as a Great Rock, and prayed that it would open. Morrison's work in the factories of the East India Company at Canton, as an interpreter, was to enable him to finally open that rock.

This was done under the most heartbreaking difficulties. During the trading season, he was compelled to live within the crowded, constricted factory site on the outskirts of Canton, whose oppressive temperature sapped every European's strength. When the merchant ships sailed, all foreigners had to leave Canton for the Portuguese colony of Macao, the only city where permanent residence was permitted. The Chinese government hunted from place to place, and sometimes seized the Chinese who cut the wooden blocks from which the first editions of the Bible were printed. The story of the production of this Bible and the accompanying grammar and dictionary embracing 4500 pages is one of dogged perseverance and courage unexcelled. Morrison was unwelcome to the Chinese, who circulated a pamphlet which read, in part: "The books that the foreigner is selling are printed with ink made of a stupefying medicine. When anyone reads them for a time, he becomes stupefied and loses his natural reason, and believes and follows the false doctrine."[7] He was unwelcome to the East India Company who wanted no trouble with the Chinese from whom they expected much profitable business. The Jesuit missionaries in Macao looked upon him as competition in an area where they had been the sole missionaries of the cross for a long time.

Although Morrison's translation was later revised many times, it, being the first Bible printed in Chinese and made available to the public, marks the beginning of the real planting of the church in China. It was this same Bible that sustained the persecuted church in China down through the years, and spoke by the Holy Spirit to the humble believer when every minister and teacher was forbidden to speak or was imprisoned. We agree with Morrison's associate, Milne, who, a few weeks before his own death, penned these words to Robert Morrison: "By God's help you have set on foot what all the empires and mandarins and priests and literati and people of China can never destroy or effectively stop..."[8] God's Word, not our opinion, is alive and powerful and alone can bring forth life everlasting in the believer.

History of Protestant Missions: 1807-1908

1807-1842 — Period of Missionary Preparation:

The period 1807 to 1842 has been called the period of missionary preparation. The war between China and Britain over the opium trade resulted in the opening of certain treaty ports.

In 1839, a large amount of opium was dumped into the sea by China in the port of Canton. In November of that year, English ships opened fire on the fleet of Admiral Kwan and with their superior ships, and fire power easily took Canton, Amoy, Ningpo, Chapel, as well as Shanghai and Chungking up the Yangtze River. The Chinese became alarmed and signed the Nanking Treaty with Great Britain. Five treaty ports were opened up where foreigners could live and carry on trade; Hong

12

Kong Island was ceded to England; a large sum of money was demanded for the loss of their opium and for waging the war.

The physical opening of these ports did not guarantee the opening of the hearts of the Chinese people to the missionaries, whom they often saw as emissaries of the imperialist, exploiting western powers. This put the missionary at a decided disadvantage and, for many years, hindered the church in its growth in China, so much so, that, up until the revolution in 1911, a convert to Christianity often lost his job and had to find employment in a mission school or hospital to earn a livelihood.

1842-1860 — Missionary Work Begins in Treaty Ports:

The years 1842 to 1860 saw the beginnings of mission work in the treaty ports. In 1841, at Peking, Hong Kong Island was ceded to the British in perpetuity after foreign troops had burned the summer palace of the Emperor. The government was forced to open their door to foreigners, both traders and missionaries.

This forcing open closed doors by military power (called gun boat diplomacy) has always hindered rather than helped the furtherance of the Kingdom of God in the long run. Treaties signed in Tientsin and Peking from 1858 to 1860 represented an even worse defeat for China than those of 1842 and 1844. Eleven more ports were opened, including Tientsin and Hankow. Western vessels were allowed access to certain inland waterways, and western missionaries and merchants were granted the right to travel about the country and to buy land.

However, the bitterness over the opium trade continued, as represented by this letter to Queen Victoria by a government official in China. He writes:

> So long as you do not take it (opium) yourselves but continue to make it and tempt the people of China to buy it, you will be showing yourselves careful of your own lives, but careless of the lives of other people; indifferent in your greed for gain to the harm you do to others. Such conduct is repugnant to human feelings and at variance with the way of heaven.
> — Signed Lin Tse-hsu[9]

1860-1880 — Opening of Interior China to Missions:

During this time the Christians found themselves at variance with the local officials of the government who felt they were guardians of Chinese culture, including their traditional religions. However, many joined churches to escape debt and judgement, as then they would come under the protection of the missionary who, as a foreign national, had extra-territorial rights, which exempted him from trial by local courts. Many of the converts in the interior were from the lower classes, as the official gentry were afraid they would lose too much in bribes if connected with Christianity. Impartial treatment in mission hospitals and schools also offended many of the gentry.

China continued to lose territory to foreign powers, other than the West, as Japan and Russia gained strength. By 1858, Kowloon on the mainland was ceded to the British. In 1860, a Sino-Russian Treaty was signed under which Ussuri (Manchuria) was ceded to the Russians. In 1876, Burma was taken by the British; in 1878, Japan took the Ryukyu Islands; in 1885, the French took Indochina; and in 1895, at the Treaty of Shimonoseki, Japan took Formosa after their successful war with China.

1880-1900 — Rapid Missionary Expansion:

From 1880 to 1900 was the period of rapid missionary expansion, especially to the West and Northeast. Mission comity was established under which each area was allotted to a mission.

By the end of the 19th century, the western powers had a vested interest in the Ch'ing dynasty, which had by then granted them so many privileges that, when the Taiping Rebellion began, the western powers lent their assistance in its suppression. This rebellion against the Manchu dynasty was led by a man who had been influenced by a distorted view of Christianity. The Taipings borrowed some things from Christianity, but the so-called god-worshippers were mainly influenced by the same peasant traditions of equality as the secret societies. They were closer to the militant aspects of the Old Testament than the living Spirit of the gospel of love. They were primarily engaged in a political and military struggle against the Manchu dynasty in Peking.

In creating Chinese armies armed and financed by the West to defeat the Taiping, the Ch'ing dynasty suffered a permanent loss of authority, as the army became the force upon which they had to depend for their power. In 1898, Kowloon north of Boundary Street, plus the New Territories, was leased to Britain for 99 years. This lease expires in 1997. Also in 1898, Kiaochou

Bay, including Tsingtao in Shangtung, was leased to Germany for 99 years. This lease was later broken by the Washington Conference. During this time that China was being exploited by foreign powers, she was also suffering internally. The Yellow River burst its dikes and flowed south, laying waste large areas. Millions of people were left homeless or dead. Epidemics of plague and cholera broke out every year in the southern provinces. Popular opposition to foreign imperialism usually found expression in hostility toward the missionaries because they were in direct contact with the Chinese people in all parts of the country. In 1891, along the Grand Canal (a man-made canal connecting Peking area with the ocean near Shanghai in the Yangtze Valley), 20 incidents took place. In these riots, plundering and looting were restricted to missions, and there was much anti-Christian propoganda. Although not many were actually killed, it was a dress rehearsal for the Boxer Rebellion. Unfortunately, many foreigners acquired the conviction that the only way to deal with the Chinese was through arms; and this kind of retaliation kindled further hostility. Many of the missionaries were kind and loved the Chinese, and were the means under God of opening schools and hospitals and churches that brought light and liberty to thousands. All their good work was ruined, however, by the arrogance and insensitivity of a few.

After China had succumbed to the Western powers by 1858, even some of the missionaries became proud and domineering. Communist historians, in later years, played up this small proportion of missionaries in their writings in order to equate the church with imperialism. Unable to defeat the power of Christ's love, manifest through His church, they put on a massive propaganda program to highlight the few who were wolves dressed in sheep's clothing.

The Boxer Rebellion
The so-called Boxers began as members of a reform movement with nationalistic dreams of the yellow race united against foreign oppression. They worshipped martial arts and skills, and claimed immunity from bullets and swords. They especially stirred up the public against the *Chinese Christians*, whom they regarded as traitors, willing to become slaves to the foreigners in return for material advantage.

During the Boxer Rebellion, there was a great slaughter of innocents, and thousands of both missionaries and national Christians and their sympathizers were slain. The foreign legations in Peking were besieged by the Boxers, who were joined by fanatic Muslims from Kansu who hated Christians; and even their former enemies, the Manchus, joined them to destroy foreigners and especially Christians.

The siege of the foreign legations in Peking began on June 20, 1900, and even the Empress Dowager urged support for this rebellion against the foreigners. With the exception of the Yuan Shih-k'ai of Shangtung and Li Hung in Canton, it seemed that the whole nation joined against the hated foreigners.

When foreign troops marched on Peking and her troops fled, Yehonola (the Manchu name of the Empress Dowager) fled to Sian, dragging the young Emperor with her. Though the Empress Dowager, Tsu Hsi, was only a concubine of the former Emperor, through stealth and cunning she became the virtual last ruler of the Manchus. Her support of the Boxers was later to prove a serious embarrassment to her, as she had done nothing to suppress it. Very vindictive terms were imposed on China, and Peking was looted and raped by the foreign troops. Some 450 million dollars worth of treasure was taken. Russians used the Boxer crisis to occupy all Manchuria. Japan sent troops to Korea, and foreign troops were stationed along the Great Wall.

The Empress Dowager finally returned from Sian with much loot and pomp, but very much humbled and forced to bow before the reform movements.

A New Day

The period from 1900 to 1911 heralded a new day for China, spiritually and politically. It was during this time that there was a mighty outpouring of the Holy Spirit upon His church worldwide. It was also the day when Sun Yat-sen, the Father of the Chinese Republic, began to stir up the people of China to revolt against the Manchu dictatorship and the corruption of the officials. Dr. Sun had become a Christian. After his salvation, he went back to his native village to show them the ineffectiveness of the idols. He did this by breaking off a finger of one of the idols, thus showing their helplessness. Because of this, he was exiled to the disgrace of his family. He went to the British colony of Hong Kong where he took a degree in medicine. After gathering support, he led an unsuccessful attack upon the 'yamen' in Canton, and was then obliged to leave the country. This was followed by years of wandering the world, absorbing ideas of constitutional government, republicanism, socialism, and also raising financial support from overseas Chinese for the growing revolt against tyranny in China. We will pick up his story later.

After the Boxer Rebellion, it seemed the whole country began to revolt against the Manchu dynasty. They were revolting, not just against a dynasty grown corrupt, but against an autocratic system which had long trodden down the masses of the people. This kind of revolt was now possible to a large degree as a result of the many schools that missionaries had opened throughout China, which taught the student to look to the future rather than to the past, contrary to Confucianism.

It was also the time of the new student volunteer movement. Elite, highly trained and educated missionaries came, and seminaries and schools multiplied. The student class in China has, from time to time, been a deciding factor. This is only natural, for the masses of the people have always reverenced the scholar and held him in high esteem. Those already in office and the military leaders did not value the students so highly, and tried to control them. In retaliation, the students turned to criticize the government. Strikes and boycotts resulted. The students invited men like Bertram Russell and John Dewey to come to China to lecture — the first time that scholars of China had invited scholars of the West to come and explain their philosophies. Unfortunately, these men were socialistic and liberal in their thinking, and influenced many students toward the left, politically.

The old dragon Queen, Empress Dowager, seeing the writing on the wall, tried to regain public support by instituting many reforms as the Manchu dynasty was about to fall. She took a positive stand against foot-binding for women. In 1905, the state examinations by which the dynasty kept its hierarchy in power were totally abolished. Manchu bands were disbanded, and the growing and using of opium was suppressed. The leaders of the revolution, both left and right, had to gain the cooperation of the foreign powers, by promising to protect them when the Manchu dynasty was overthrown. By then, the foreign powers had much land and many concessions and privileges in China, and were trying to hold onto them. It was a time

17

of great peril in China. In the year 1908 the Empress Dowager died just a few days after her nephew, Emperor Kwang Hsu had died, (many suspected that her hatred for him prompted her to see to it that he died before her). A very elaborate funeral, costing millions, was held for her, far outshining the funeral of the Emperor. It was the celebration of the death of the old dynasties.

War Lord Era

Then began the era of the war lords. Veritable feudal lords, backed by large armies, they made and unmade government officials. They collected and established taxes, levied new ones, seized railroad revenues. They early found that opium revenues brought them more easy money than anything else. So they encouraged its growth. Sometimes they confiscated the same crop from the hapless farmer they had previously forced him to plant at the point of the gun. Often long lines of soldiers of this and that War Lord escorted the carriers of the opium to the big shipping centers. The opium habit, which had been largely stamped out during the Empress Dowager's days, was again fastened upon the people. This is not to say that all the War Lords were bad, some truly had the welfare of the people at heart.

Three War Lords were in virtual control of the most of China. Wu-pei-fu was a well-educated man of military training, possessing courage and ambition. Chang Tso-lin was of a rougher sort; had served in the Japanese army; was taken into the Chinese army in Manchuria, and had become dictator of the province. Lastly, Feng Yu-siang, a professing Christian, but without education, maintained strict discipline of his troops and taught them bits of the Bible. As his army marched, they sang "Onward Christian Soldiers."

Revolution

On October 9, 1911, a bomb in a revolutionary house in Wuchang exploded, forcing a band of revolutionaries to stage a rebellion in order to save their lives. Thus, the students and revolutionary-inclined patriots, who had not felt strong enough up until that time, were forced into action. They quickly took Hankow, Wuchang (twin cities) and Hanyang. The Manchus were not ready to meet the situation, and there was little warfare or destruction. Each province, in turn, deserted the dynasty and aligned itself on the revolutionary side. The rebels put cities under military rule, and armed pickets patrolled the streets. When days went by and no slaughter nor violence occurred, the people who had fled the cities went back into the cities and went about their old occupations. Soldiers, armed with large shears, stood at the city gates on important thoroughfares. A snap of the shears as a man with a queue passed, and the mark of bondage to the Manchus disappeared.

One of the results of revolution was language reform. Up until this time, the Wen Li, or the classical language of the scholars was the only official written language. This differed widely from the spoken language. The idea of borrowing the characters from the Wen Li, but following the form of the spoken language was proposed. The spoken language most common to the 18 provinces was the Mandarin, and they endeavored to make it the national language. It was not until 1928, however, that school texts in the Wen Li were abolished and were written in the Kuo Yu or Mandarin from that time onward. The communists have since further simplified the characters so that many of the common people can read and write now. Almost all young people, 30 years old and under, can now speak the Kuo Yu, the national language, or Mandarin, which is quite an accomplishment for a land of one billion people.

Up to now, we have been looking mostly at the outward workings of the Dragon Kingdom up until the death throes of the last of the dynasties. However, underneath this outward battle a real spiritual battle has been going on for the souls of one-quarter of the world's population. Although the Nationalists still celebrate the tenth day of the tenth month as liberation day, many are not free at all.

In the next chapter, as we examine the life of one of those sent by God to plant the church of the cross where the dragon has reigned, we will see how God chose the weak things of the world to overcome the mighty.

Chapter III

The Dragon Fighter

Enter The Knight — Ivan Kauffman

In legend, it is the knight in shining armor that slays the dragon with his magical sword. In reality, God uses ordinary men with extraordinary faith. "...but God has chosen the foolish things of the world to shame the wise, and God has chosen the weak things of the world to shame the things which are strong...that no man should boast before God" (1 Corinthians 1:27, 29 NASB). But God does not send the weak man out alone. He says, "Go, and lo I am with you always." He gives him the whole armor of God and asks him to take in his had the Sword of the Spirit, which is the Word of God, the Word which, by its power, formed the universe out of nothing (Hebrews 11:3).

The story I want to tell is about just such an ordinary man who, under God, did extraordinary things.

The year was 1908. The dragon Queen had just died. It was a time when, in China, every man did that which was right in his own eyes. Warlords and bandits ruled the land.

Just as God sent the young man, Robert Morrison, one hundred years before to prepare that Sword of the Spirit so that every one of the 400 million Chinese could relate to it, so now God sent an ordinary young man into the fray to wield that Sword in the power of the Spirit.

As our story opens, we see a young man in his early twenties on horseback riding over the precipitous paths of the remote mountains of Northwest China near the borders of Tibet. Although he is dressed in the same Chinese padded garments as those in the mule train (to keep them warm in this high, rarefied atmosphere), his face stands out very white in contrast to those of the swarthy orientals around him. He is short of stature, but strong and wiry, with muscles made strong hoeing the corn and plowing the fields of his father's farm in America. The crow's

20

feet at the corners of his eyes reveal a sense of humour that give him a zest for life and the ability to face dangers seen and unseen. The strong, straight Roman nose, contrasting so with the flat noses of the men around him, was donated by his Pennsylvania Dutch background. His ancestors came from Switzerland in the early 1700's to what was later to be called Pennsylvania, or Penn's woods. They were deeply religious, having been influenced by men like Count Zinzendorf of the Moravians and Menno Simons, founder of the Mennonites. They had come to the new world searching for freedom to worship God as they felt they should. The man spurs his horse and races ahead of the plodding mules to catch his first glimpse of the forbidden land of Tibet, its snow-capped Himalayan Mountains acting as a formidable barrier to the gospel.

Tibet

In the land of the dragon many ethnic groups have mingled to create what we know as the Chinese. The Han Chinese inhabited the best agricultural land, leaving the mountains, steppes, and other less desirable regions to the national minorities (many of whom are pastoralists). The Mongols in the north, Turkic peoples in the northwest, Tibetans in the west and southwest, and Tai peoples in the south are the principal groups. Of all the principal non-Han peoples inhabiting China's frontier regions, the Tibetans were perhaps the most isolated and most backward. It was here, also, that the dragon reigned supreme. An oppressive feudal system, in which the Tibetan Lamas held political and religious sway over the serfs under them, had kept the people in fear and bondage for centuries. Tibetan Lamaism is a blend of Mahayana Buddhism and the Tibetan animistic beliefs known as Bon. The Monks or Lamas comprised one-sixth of the population. For instance, the Dreprung Monastery housed over 10,000 monks. Every family sent at least one son into the priesthood. But these monks, besides being trained in Buddhism, were taught to worship demons. Fasting and chanting the overtones of "O-mami-pat-mi-hum" for hours, until the demons would materialize before their eyes, and then becoming possessed by them, was part of their worship. As he advanced on these ranges, behind which a whole race of people was held in Satanic sway by this Lamaistic Heirarchy, he was literally bearding the dragon in his den. This young, poorly educated farm boy from Pennsylvania, going out to meet the

21

enemy of mankind, must be out of his mind. Yes, it seemed foolish, but "...the foolishness of God is wiser than men, and the weakness of God is stronger than men" (1 Corinthians 1:25 NASB).

I got to know this dragon fighter quite well, you see, for he was my father, and I would like to tell you his story and the story of the maid that God sent into his life; and how God used one who was least in the Kingdom of God to influence the great land of China in a way that only eternity will reveal.

Nyak

Ivan Saunders Kauffman was born on February 17, 1885 in Sporting Hill, Pennsylvania, the eldest son of Isaac and Elizabeth Kauffman. Isaac was a Pennsylvania Dutch farmer, road builder and jack-of-all-trades, and a popular speaker at all occasions. He was a popular figure in the community, and his story-telling ability was praised at the local town hall. Ivan was the eldest of seven children, two of whom died early. In order to help support the family, Ivan left school when quite young to work in a cigar factory. At the age of 17, being tired of the small town and its narrow ways, he set out to make his fortune in the big city of New York. As this young country boy walked down the hill from his home town toward Lititz with his battered suitcase, dressed in his best stiff celluloid collar and black shiny suit, the angels in heaven were watching. The Lord, who knows the hearts of all men, knowing that Ivan had come to the cross-roads of his life, moved upon the heart of his servant, Daddy Brubaker. Reverend Brubaker was General Manager of the Christian and Missionary Alliance Missionary Training Institute in Nyak, New York. He was home in Lititz on his vacation and, seeing the young lad coming down the hill, he rose to meet him. He said, "Ivan, where are you going?" Ivan said, "To find a job in the big city." Daddy Brubaker said, "How would you like to work for us at the Nyak Bible School on the Hudson? We need a hard-working young man. How about it?" Ivan said, "I would like to give it a try." So, through a seemingly chance meeting, a missionary dynasty was born.

Conversion

He was first employed as a stoker in the boiler room where he kept things hopping. Knowing his reputation for fearlessness, one of the students dared him to climb the tall chimney of the boiler room. Not only did he take the dare, but, in the bargain, he stood on his head on the top. Such was the nature of the man God was preparing to carry the gospel where angels almost feared to tread. The students soon took a liking to him and began to pray for him, and, before long, he came under the convicting power of the Holy Spirit and found the Lord as his Saviour. He then entered the Institute as a student, working part-time.

Call

The year was 1903, and the modern day Pentecostal revival was sweeping the world. At Nyak, under Dr. A. B. Simpson, the students began to humble themselves and seek the face of God for an infilling of the Holy Spirit. Let me quote from an old friend of Ivan's, Frank Edmond, who was present.

Brother Ivan was shown by God such an awful picture of his sin that he sought to hide in the attic of the Institute under some old quilts. For two days he could not be found, and when the furnaces began to burn down, a big search was made, and he was found in the attic in deep soul agony. Out of this deep heart-searching the Lord revealed Himself to him as Sanctifier and Baptiser in the Holy Ghost and fire, according to Acts 2:4. At that time God called him to China. After that, he was lost to all else, for his heart was always in China.[10]

Preparation

After graduation from Nyak in 1908, he and Victor Plymire, another Pennsylvania Dutchman, along with a senior missionary of the Christian and Missionary Alliance, set out for the most remote and difficult mission field in the world at that time — Tibet.

Crossing the sea, however, does not make a missionary and, before he began his missionary work overseas, he went home. As he witnessed to his mother, whose heart was tender to the things of God, she yielded her life to Christ right away. But Isaac Kauffman was a proud man. When his young son began to witness to him, he stormed out of the house went down to the local tavern to try and ease the conviction of sin in his heart with strong drink. That night, as he wove his way home, suddenly, like Saul of Tarsus, the Lord spoke so plainly to him that he called out for mercy. When he got home, although the hour was late, he found both son Ivan and Mother praying for his salvation, and they had a camp meeting of their own. Isaac Kauffman went on to become a lay preacher in the "United Zion Church." His gift as a speaker, now anointed by the Holy Spirit, was used of God to bring the gospel to many in that community.

The Mission and the Man
After the long journey of a month across the Pacific, seasick most of the way, they arrived in Shanghai. From there they went up the Yangtze River by boat to Hankow. On the way to Hankow, the rope, with which the porters pulled one of the boats up the strong current, broke. In the boat was much of the outfit that they had taken with them. It was swept down onto the rocks and overturned. They had to stop and dry out the items before they could continue on their way. From Hankow, by train to the end of the line and then by mule cart at first and then horseback, it took them three months from the end of the railroad before they reached their mission station of Taojofu in Kansu Province on the border of Tibet.

Others who knew him said that Ivan Kauffman was a very humble man, one who liked to get alone to pray often. He took misunderstanding and even cruelty to his person with a Christ-like spirit. But he was also a fearless and fine athlete. The Tibetans were very fond of wrestling and were tall, well-built men with sinewy muscles developed from carrying heavy loads up the mountain trails of the Himalayas. Ivan Kauffman was short, just a few inches over five feet, but more than one Tibetan, in a friendly wrestling match, found himself flat on his back, for what Ivan lacked in height and weight, he made up in agility and speed. His ability as a horseman, an art held in high esteem in that society, was soon known in the region. He was a crack shot with a rifle. He had brought with him a Winchester repeater. To the tribesmen of Tibet, it seemed like a weapon from outerspace, for they still used the clumsy flintlocks. He was able to bring down wild game, such as deer and pheasant, to replenish the larder of both missionary and national alike. In that barren region, the yak was the main source of meat and milk, and only a few vegetables, such as potatoes and carrots, could be grown. They never saw fresh fruit. A pack train would sometimes bring some frozen persimmons by pack mule over the mountain trails as a special treat. Once, knowing that they were having some visitors, Ivan was planning to surprise them with some homemade ice cream. The rich yak milk was collected and the cream skimmed off, and he found a mountain cave where ice had formed. He was hard at work churning the ice cream freezer when the board on which he was working slipped, and the whole thing spilled on the ground. What a disappointment!

The Tibetans entertained guests by serving them a special tea into which rancid yak butter had been placed and stirred around with little balls of barley flour called Tsamba. This, to them, was a delicacy, and Ivan got so he was able to swallow it without making a face. Because of these several reasons, the nationals found in him a real friend. He always had time for their needs and problems, and no effort was too great. Many times he was called out of bed at night to ride on horseback over the mountains to try and stop the bleeding and stitch up the wound of a Tibetan who had been the loser in a fight. Every Tibetan carried a heavy sword and used it at the slightest provocation.

He always carried his trusty forceps for extracting teeth. There were few dentists in that region, and he was able to relieve many a toothache by simply pulling out the infected tooth, and the Lord, in answer to prayer, made it possible that he never lost a patient. Once, when they were having some tent meetings in a marketplace to preach the gospel, a Chinese acrobatic company opened close to them. When the people heard the clanging of the cymbals and the high, harsh notes of the sackbut, they all began to rush out of the meeting. Ivan called them back and promised to show them something no one in the acrobatic troupe could do. When they all sat down, he took out his false teeth with a flourish and then, to their amazement, put them in again and smiled a toothy grin to prove that he could still use them. He had their attention for the rest of the meeting.

Spiritual Warfare

In those days the term was seven or eight years, and there were no trips back by jet to see your family, no matter what the emergency. The loneliness and hardships of those days can only be imagined. The religion of the Tibetans, as we have mentioned, was none other than demon worship. When they gathered for seasons of chanting and dancing, the demons would materialize before their eyes, and one could tell from the demeanor of the spirit whether it was a spirit of lust, hatred or pride. All kinds of demon possession were rampant, and Ivan was glad that the Lord had led him into the baptism of the Holy Spirit which gave him boldness and power to bring deliverance in Jesus' Name to many who were thus possessed with demons, if they desired to be set free.

The first place they were able to purchase as a chapel and dwelling had been a former Lamasery. The first night in the place taught them the reality of the powers of darkness. They didn't sleep a wink, and one of the missionary wives said she could actually feel the demons breathing down her neck. It took days of fasting and prayer before the place was exorcised of demons and they could sleep there and have their meetings. From a place where demons were worshipped, it became a house of prayer and worship to the Lord Jesus through the power of His Name!

Spiritual warfare took many other forms on that frontier. White Wolf, a famous bandit chief, was rampaging in the countryside. Hearing of the Western missionaries now living in the old monastery, he decided to attack and capture them for ransom. An old Chinese woman, who had found Christ as her Saviour, heard of his plan and ran to warn them. The Chinese government had dispatched some soldiers to guard the westerners, but, when they heard the White Wolf and his band were on the way, they ran and hid for fear. As the little company knelt in prayer, the peace of God filled their hearts. On opening their eyes, their eyes fell on the Winchester repeaters hanging on the wall. A number of the missionaries had brought them with them. Feeling that this was to be their means of deliverance, they took them down and loaded them. As the bandit band came up the mountain pass, confident in their boldness, they were surprised to see the flashes of rifle fire coming from almost every window of the fortress-like monastery. The missionaries were running from window to window, firing their automatic rifles over the heads of the advancing horde as fast as possible. The bandits thought that a whole army of Chinese soldiers were guarding them and turned tail and fled. Even though they heard later of the way they were tricked, the loss of precious face to them was so great that they never tried to do it again. In the confusion of darknesss of the night, one of the bandits, however, was killed, and that death of the one to whom Ivan had come to preach the love of Jesus would haunt him for a long time to come.

The women and children and all the Christians of that area did, however, praise God for His protection and care over them, and rejoiced at the fulfillment of the promise that "two shall put ten thousand to flight" (Deuteronomy 32:30) when accompanied by the Lord of Hosts.

The Spirit of God, who was moving around the world at that time, was also moving in Tibetan country. As Ivan Kauffman learned the gutteral Tibetan language and with his fellows began to preach the gospel, the Spirit of God worked with them with signs following. Every soul saved was a brand snatched from the burnings of hell, and the enemy contested every inch of ground. But, wherever the Holy Spirit found honest, hungry hearts, He met them. Soon a company of Spirit-filled believers was raised up, and men like W. W. Simpson and Victor Plymire became fire brands to spread the fire of the gospel in that remote part of the world, shoulder to shoulder with Ivan Kauffman.

This Pentecostal fire was not received by all with like enthusiasm. Both missionaries and national pastors opposed it with determination. It was called fanaticism. Someone has defined a fanatic as someone who is just a little more fanatic than you are. Nevertheless, it was termed wild fire by many very orthodox missionaries, and these Pentecostal men were more or less ostracized by their fellow workers.

Furlough Time

The Robert Eckvals, who worked with Ivan there in Taojo, had suffered greatly in that spiritual battle. They lost three little ones whom they buried in the lonely hills of the Tibetan border within the space of one week with fever. It fell to Ivan's lot, as the single missionary, to make the three rough wooden coffins, place the remains of the three little ones in them, and bury them in Taojofu where the only graveyard was. Mrs. Eckval had a complete nervous breakdown and, as is so often the case, didn't want any close relatives near her. The year was 1916. China, still under the rule of the warlords, hung in the balance, having not yet decided to enter the Great War against Germany and her allies, and already harboring in her bosom many who sympathized with the revolution in the Soviet Union. Ivan Kauffman was asked to take Mrs. Eckval down to the coast and home along with another lady missionary for her companion. As the ship again sailed near to his native land, he had many momentous decisions to make. He had to decide whether to give up the Pentecostal message and go with the Christian and Missionary Alliance who, since A. B. Simpson's death, had come out very strongly against the message. Or if not, he would have to trust the Lord for His complete support, as he had no local church of any size behind him, and his heart was still in China. Much time was spent on his face before the Lord for guidance.

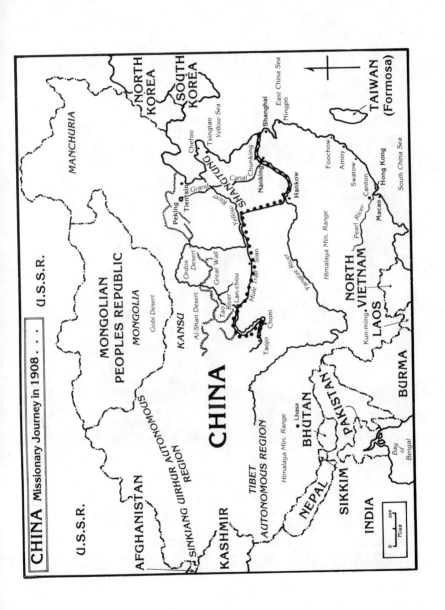

1. Traveling by "Shanza" in N.W. China – 1917

2. Typical Chinese Inn on Journey to Taojo.

3. Mountain Road to Taojo.

4. Frances and first born son at Taojo – 1918

5. Taojo saints, both Chinese, Tibetan and missionary.

6. Springless mule cart caravan to Taojo.

7. First Church in Tsingtao, Peking Rd. – 1924.

8. Welcome for Frances after returning from Hong Kong widowed – taken at Tsingtao docks, – 1934 – Bro & Sis. George Kelley beside her.

9. Faithful Chinese Pastors and Bible Women. Tsingtao.

10. Ivan studying Tibetian on border of Tibet 1908.

11. Baptismal service on beach in Tsingtao 1928.

12. National workers and families in Tsingtao in 1928.

13. Frances Thompson 1908.

14. Ivan Kauffman 1908.

15. Frances and Ivan just married – 1917.

16. Kauffman family – 1923.

17. Kauffman family – 1925.

18. Kauffman family – 1933.

19. Ivan Kauffman 1929.

20. Frances Kauffman 1947.

21. **Frances at Ivan's grave at Happy Valley, Hong Kong 1937.**

22. **Sleeping Buddha Idol.**

23. Rev. and Mrs. Isaac Kauffman
(Father and mother of Ivan) 1943.

24. Tibetan Priest with prayer wheel.

25. Inside The Forbidden City, Peking.

26. Entrance to Ming Tombs, Don and Paul Kauffman.

27. Great Wall.

28. In front of #6 Hunan Road. Tsingtao – our old home – 1979.

29. Hall in Tsingtao in which services were held during revival. – 1930.

30. At Tien An gate, Peking – 1979. (Mongolian maiden in foreground).

31. Oct. 1 Communists celebrating Mao's red book.

32. Potala, Dalai-Lamaś Palace, with 1,000 rooms, Lhasa, Tibet.

Chapter IV

The Maid

Enter The Maid — Frances Jean Thompson

At this point in the story, we will let Frances Kauffman, my mother, tell what happened firsthand, from her own lips. Frances Kauffman Buchwalter went to her reward only in February 1980 and has left us the following account, in writing and on tape, of what happened when Ivan arrived on furlough in 1916. I have filled in some gaps from letters and periodicals.

They had met in Nyak where Ivan had roomed for one year with Omar Buchwalter, who was to marry Frances twenty years after Ivan Kauffman had been called to his reward.

Mother recalls:

"Ivan had written me that he was returning home, but the letter did not arrive until he, himself, arrived on the shores of America. He first returned home to Lancaster County in Pennsylvania to visit his parents. He found that the Pentecostal movement that had just begun when he was last there had become a mighty force in the church in America. Men like H. H. Cox, W. I. Evans, Frank Boyd and Oswald Flower had been filled with the Spirit, and were becoming leaders in a new movement called the Assemblies of God. In Lancaster, along with some of the Buchwalter family, old friends of ours from Bible school, he began to assist in the newly founded Assembly which later became the First Assembly of God church in Lancaster, Pennsylvania. The Lord used Ivan to help many of the believers in the assembly there to open up to the Holy Spirit and be filled with the Spirit, with the initial evidence of speaking in other tongues.

"As soon as he could get away, he came up to Toronto, partly to see me, as we had become engaged to be married, and partly because of an invitation from Rev. H. L. Stephens of Nyak, and the so-called Robert Street Mission, a Pentecostal

Holiness church pastored by Rev. A. G. Ward, who had recently come out of one of the older historical denominations as they would not condone the experience of the baptism with the Holy Spirit which he had received. Ivan and Brother Ward became life-long friends. A. G. Ward said, "I have long believed that, if one lives for half a century and makes one true friend, he need not complain. Ivan Kauffman was, in our judgement, a true, intimate friend. We understood each other and had many interests in common."[11] Through the depression years in China, when often the missions department of The Pentecostal Assemblies of Canada, of which A. G. Ward became missionary secretary, could not send very much support, their friendship was surely tried and tested, but this strong bond lasted until death. Ivan along with some of the Robert Street Church group started a new mission called the Hebdon Mission in downtown Toronto. This became Evangel Temple, which later bought the old Congregational Church at Bond and Dundas.

"But, before I launch into the story of our life together, let me give my testimony. I was raised in a home where we were taught to beware of people who called themselves Christians. My father was a travelling salesman and had met many who bore the name of Christ, but whose hearts had never been changed. As a small child, I was permitted to go to Sunday School with other children and, thank God, we had a fine young teacher who knew the Lord and had a passion for souls. It was through her that I was led to give my heart to Jesus at the age of thirteen. Two very dear friends of those early days in Toronto have been so faithful and kind. Both of them have gone home to heaven, but I want to mention their names and give thanks to the Lord for them. They were Ethel McDonald and Mame Ashling. Along with my Sunday School teacher, I prayed daily for the salvation of my parents. Father finally yielded to Christ at the age of fifty-five. As he knelt before the Lord, he prayed, "If you'll take the remains of a ruined life, Christ, I'll come." The remaining eight years of his life were a living testimony of the power of God to set a man free from tobacco and from bad language. He daily exorted others to yield to Christ while they were young. Although my mother was religious, it was not until just before her death that she yielded her life to Jesus. Rev. A. G. Ward was the one who led her in the prayer that brought her into the family of God.

Marriage

"On July 22, in the year 1917, Ivan Saunders Kauffman and I, Frances Jean Thompson, were united in holy matrimony at the Anglican church, 661 Dufferin Street, Toronto. We were mature adults, Ivan being 32 and having completed one eight year term in China, on the border of Tibet, and I was 28. I had completed my training at Nyak and back in Toronto had taken a nursing-at-home training course of practical nursing to prepare for the mission field, a course which I was to appreciate so much later on.

Like Abraham

"Very soon after our marriage, we set faces toward Tibet with our eyes on the Lord of Calvary. We did not have any substantial continuing support aside from a few love offerings, such as from the Robert Street Mission. Like Abraham, we set out not knowing how far we would be able to go. We had enough money for the train fare to the next railroad stop where we knew some Pentecostal believers. Thus, from place to place we worked our way across the continent. When we arrived in Chicago, we were invited to speak at the Stone Church, one of the First Assembly of God Churches to be opened in the United States. Here a Miss Riff felt led of God to provide enough money for the remainder of our journey to Tibet and also to help us with our outfit. With this direct confirmation from the Lord, we started out. The Pentecostal Assemblies of Canada churches, having just begun and having not been chartered with the government, could only stand behind us in prayer, but as soon as possible would pledge to send us some monthly support. Both the Assemblies of God in the U.S. and the Pentecostal Assemblies of Canada were raised up by God to be missionary movements at the very first. Much home missions work remained to be done, and many were meeting in homes and store fronts and had no church buildings of their own. But the Holy Spirit directed the hearts of those who were baptized in the Holy Spirit to reach out to those that were in complete heathen darkness overseas. This spiritual principle of "give and it shall be given" has been the secret of the growth of this comparatively new movement. If they ever lose this missionary vision, they will begin to die.

"The long trip across the vast expanse of the Pacific, being tossed by the huge waves, brought us to Shanghai and our first glimpse of China. The noisy, jostling Chinese coolies, who vied for the privilege of carrying our baggage for a few copper coins, was a foretaste of the millions of this great land who hunger and reach out for the crumbs from the Master's table. While we feast at the full table in our own land, so many have never once heard.

Travel In China — Circa 1917

"We took the boat up the swift Yangtze gorges pulled by the porters whose bare feet had worn deep ruts in the rocks along the shore by centuries of sweat and toil. Then by crowded train to the end of the line we travelled. From then on we took to the springless mule cart. The roads in this area were through the loess dust which had been blown from the Gobi Desert and covered the earth. The mules had worn deep valleys through which we travelled. The heat and the dust soon changed our colour until we appeared the same dusty gray that everyone else looked like. The only way our colour was given away was when the sweat washed the dust away or my brown hair was exposed. We, in those days, also wore the same Chinese gowns as the Chinese did. As we moved through the valleys, carved through the loess by centuries of mule trains that have travelled these trade routes of West China, I could not help but remember our lovely home in the fashionable residential area of Gladstone Avenue in Toronto where everything was so clean and every speck of dust was soon wiped up by our maid. At night we stopped at the Inns and slept on the hollow mud "kongs" which, in the cold weather, had a fire built under them. These hard beds were covered with coarse, vermin-ridden horsehair mats. Perhaps someone with leprosy had slept on the same mat the night before. In the cool evenings yak chips were burned under the hollow 'kongs' for warmth. One side almost burned to a turn, while the other side was cold as one looked up through the roof and saw the stars, as many of the roof tiles had been blown off by the fierce desert winds.

"At the end of the road the way became a narrow trail winding high into the Himalaya ranges. My husband did fine as he rode horseback, but they put me into a 'shanza' (a basket on two poles slung between two mules that walked single file and knew nothing about keeping in step.) I had lice day and night as the bedding in the 'shanza' was put on the 'kong' at the Inn at night. A welcome relief in the long five months' journey should have been to stop at a friendly mission station where one could finally take off one's vermin-ridden clothes and have a hot bath and have one's clothes washed and ridden of vermin for a time, at least. But word had gone out to the mission stations, and even this small relief was denied us.

The Reproach of Pentecost

"The missions were told that these tongues-speaking people were bringing false doctrine, and they were not to bid them Godspeed. I took deathly sick and they had to carry me from the 'shanza' to the dirty 'kong' bed. I lay on the mud 'kong', no longer noticing the lice that covered my body, and prepared for death. One of the muleteers happened to meet a missionary on the street and told him that one of his own kind was dying in the Inn, and that he had better go down and see her. The missionary, whose name was Lloyd Rist, had known me and, in fact, his sisters were good friends, having also attended Nyak. They had been told to have nothing to do with us, but when the news of my condition came to him, he rushed down to the Inn. When he saw me in my pitiful condition, he burst into tears and said, "God forgive us. Do you call this the love of God?" They took me into their home and bathed me and nursed me until my recovery. Ivan, however, had to go on with the caravan of goods. One had to take supplies, such as flour and sugar and kerosene, and the muleteers had been hired for the journey. So, knowing that I was in good hands, he went on, promising to return for me as soon as he could. Lloyd Rist, himself, was to come down with typhus from the bite of a louse some years later, and went to his reward, leaving his wife in that barren country. The love and care they showed to one of His little ones will be rewarded throughout eternity, I am sure.

"Ivan finally returned, and rejoiced to see me well again. After thanking the Rists and praying God's blessing on them, we set off for Taojo, our mission station destination.

The Newlyweds' First Home

"A Chinese gentleman had recently built a large house from the wood of the old monastery. You remember Ivan telling about how the Lord delivered them from the White Wolf and his band in that old monastery. The bandits had said later that every window was lighted and a soldier was at every window. As a result of this defeat to their pride and loss of face, they threatened to kill Ivan if he dared to return. Well, here he was, and he had also brought me, his newly wedded bride, with him. We rented one floor of this big house. Under us, on the ground floor, was the stable with the horses, yak, etc. But it was home, and I soon had it looking much more comfortable.

"It was a lonely life up there. Ivan was away, often for weeks at a time, travelling into Tibetan country. I longed for the companionship of my own kind. I could not walk by myself. A large Tibetan dog, the size of a calf, guarded the door and, whenever I went out, I had to have a male servant walk with me to guard me. Besides a large sword, he also carried a long pole. In this part of the country, the Tibetans do not bury their dead, but throw the bodies on the mountainside or into the river for the buzzards to dispose of. Our house was situated beside the Tao River on one side and a high mountain on the other. The long pole was for the purpose of pushing the dead bodies out into the stream, for, often they would become caught in small eddies on the shore. Such was the scenery that surrounded us. It was wild and grand with snowcapped mountains, but it was also marred by fallen man. At times, I was asked to go to visit someone who was sick or had been wounded in tribal fights, and my nurse's training came in very handy.

Beauty

"Ivan had a very high-spirited, high-stepping horse named Beauty. When Ivan was on his back, he often reared up on his hind legs and showed the whites of his eyes, and then raced, with mane flying, over the dangerous mountain trails as sure-footed as a mountain goat. But when I got on his back, his nature changed completely. He seemed to know, by some sixth sense, that I was expecting our first child, and he walked along as gently as a lamb. Some months later, Ivan, unfortunately, lost his prize horse. It happened like this. It was the custom to take a gift with one when making a visit. Ivan was asked to visit the local magistrate to pay his respects. The gift was, in this instance, really a bribe that was supposed to insure special treatment and protection. Knowing this, he did not take a gift, but only presented a Bible to the magistrate. The magistrate seemed to be pleased, although he was a heathen man. When Ivan was about to leave and was bowing out, the magistrate said again, "Thank you for the wonderful gift you have brought for me. I really appreciate it and will see that you are well treated in the district from now on." Still rather puzzled, Ivan went out in the courtyard to get his horse. Instead of the horse, he was met by bowing, smiling attendants of the magistrate who thanked Ivan for the gift of the high-stepping horse. Complaining would have made matters much worse, so he just had to accept matters as they were and get another horse. But he never again found as high-spirited nor yet as gentle a horse as old faithful Beauty.

First Child

"My time soon came when I was to be delivered of my first child. The nearest doctor and hospital was seven days' journey over the mountain passes. But just 50 Chinese "li" from us in the city of Choni lived the McGillivrays. Mrs. McGillivray was trained as a midwife in England, and she offered to help me at the birth of our child. Old Beauty took me safely there. When the labor started, it was very difficult. With no anaesthetic nor instruments, it was doubly hard. But as they prayed together, after two days of hard labor, finally a five pound baby boy, whom we named Donald was born, with great praise to God. I was very weak after the ordeal, so I had to stay on in Choni to rest for a while, while Ivan went back to his mission station in Taojo. A very mysterious disease began to break out in the Tibetan Monastery across from where they lived in Choni. Under the Lama system, each family must give one of their sons to the monastery for training, and many of these little boys who went there at the age of 12 were deathly sick. The McGillivrays also took sick, and I, though still very weak, was asked to go to the monastery to try to help them and also to nurse the missionaries. We now know that this was the dreaded flu epidemic that swept the world after the First World War. There were no doctors for miles around. The little Tibetan boy, who was our servant, kept a little wood fire burning in the room and milked the yak. There were no cows in that high altitude of some 14,000 feet, but the long-haired, hardy little yak produced rich, nourishing milk that kept my little boy alive, as I was too weak to breast-feed him.

"In the meantime, Ivan, who was also busy trying to help to nurse the many who were dying of the plague in Taojo, himself took sick. His little Chinese boy servant kept a can of water boiling on the stove, and it was all the medicine he received. Back in Choni, having no way of getting news from him, I waited for his return and, at times, thought he had been killed by bandits who infested these mountain passes. There were runners who could be employed to take messages, but this was not available during the plague. When he finally came riding back on his faithful horse, thin and pale, but alive, there was a joyful reunion.

"The problem was how to get me and the baby back to Taojo, as I was still very weak. The high altitude and the long, hard labor had taken its toll. Unable to eat much of the local food, I had lost much weight also. Finally, Mr. McGillivray made arrangements for the Choni Prince, who was a rich land-owner, to send over his sedan chair which he used for state occasions. With it came 30 stalwart sedan chair bearers. Fifteen men carried the large, elaborate chair, taking turns spelling one another off every fifteen minutes as the chair was so heavy. This frail, little missionary lady, with her frail, but lively little baby boy, was treated like royalty on our way back to Taojo.

Back Home In Taojo

"It was good to be back in our own rooms. I remember, in going up to them, we had to pass two coffins of the Chinese couple who owned the house. It was Chinese custom to pur-chase and keep in a prominent place one's coffin before death, especially if they were expensive and well-made of thick, stout wood as a sign of one's wealth and position in society. But, for the grace of God, we both could have been in a coffin, perhaps not quite as elaborate. Bro. W. W. Simpson's son, Robert, who had been brought up in this Tibetan area and spoke like a native, was tragically killed by bandits as he went down to meet his father who was coming back on furlough from the U.S. a few years later. Many graves of those whose lives were given to take the gospel to these needy people will burst wide open at the resurrection morning and these martyrs will rejoice with those who have come to know Jesus through their witness. In later years, Bro. Plymire told of some 40 assemblies in this frontier area. The first two were planted in Taojo, and the seed grew and brought forth much fruit.

"Death was everywhere present as bandits and warlords fought back and forth over this valley. The plague took the lives of thousands. One would often see fences around a monastery made of human bones of those who had died in the plague, and their bones, after having been stripped clean by wild animals and vultures, were put to good use and were a gruesome reminder of the shortness of life in this cruel country.

"When Donald was just a few months old, one night there was a pounding at the door of the home. The gate keeper, after letting the horseman in to refresh himself, came to tell Ivan that a woman was dying in childbirth, and asked if I could come and help. It was a bitter cold night, and he was loath to let me go out in my still weakened condition. But, after dressing in the warm fleece-lined Chinese gown and having prayer, I got on horseback and was led over the mountains to a young lady who had been a patient in the Alliance hospital in Lanchou. It was her firstborn, and the custom was to go back home for the birth of the first child. There were serious complications in the birth, and she had already been in labor many hours. After much prayer and thanking the Lord for my midwifery course in the nurse's training in Toronto, I was able to deliver a baby boy. They asked me to bathe the little one with oil, as was the custom in the American hospital. They gave me two bottles that the hospital had given to her. The label on one said carbolic acid and, on the other, oil for bathing. As I was trained to do, I automatically poured a little from the bottle labelled "oil" into the palm of my hand and smelled it. It immediately began to burn my hand, as it was carbolic acid. As I bathed the little son of this local magistrate in the oil from the other bottle, I lifted my heart in thanksgiving to the Lord who had been with me and saved the life of this little babe.

It's Not An Easy Road

"As I went out on the mountainside, and the servant carried little Donald on his back beside me, I used to sing, "I'll go where You want me to go, dear Lord, over mountain or plain or sea." The safe, warm church hall of the Robert Street Church in Toronto would come into my mind's eye. I wondered, if I had known what I know now, whether I would have sung that song at the altar with such zest or not. I learned, however, that God gives grace when it is needed and not before. As we follow Him, He will give grace and glory.

"When I got home, I would have to take the little babe from the servant and search the bedding for body lice. You see, the Tibetans never killed them as, "who knows," they said, "you might be killing your ancestor." So strong was their belief in reincarnation. They ate little meat, and many died of famine, being surrounded by herds of yak, much as in the pitiful land of India. How Satan had blinded their eyes, and these noble people were being destroyed by him. As the light of the gospel came to them, what joy filled their hearts and what joy filled our hearts, and we praised the Lord for His grace that had enabled us to answer the call of God to go to the uttermost parts of the earth.

"After two years on the border of Tibet, because of my ill health, we had to return to Canada. On the return journey to the coast, the same filthy Inns and springless mule carts were the instruments of torture that proved the dedication of the pioneer missionaries. Often, in the Inn at night, if the vermin did not keep you awake, the braying of the donkeys and mules would. And, looking up at the stars through the broken roof, thoughts of home and the clean, sweet smelling sheets would drift into one's mind. But, on the other hand, the joyful faces of hundreds that would not have met Jesus Christ face to face and that would not have been delivered from the fear of death and an eternity of endless rebirth, more than compensated for any small discomfort which lasted but for a moment. The journey back to Canada was without incident, as we had now become seasoned travellers.

Furlough

"While visiting Ivan's parents near Lancaster, the time came for the birth of our second son, Paul. His birth brought great joy to our hearts. The experience of birth in the General Hospital in Lancaster was very different to the birth on the border of Tibet. After a time of rest in Canada, we visited the churches of the Pentecostal Assemblies of Canada, which had now become organized into a Fellowship, registered with the government and with their Missions Department, of which R. E. McAlister was the first missionary secretary. We again felt the pull of the Spirit to return to China. The situation in China was very troubled, as the Communist Party, with Mao Tse-tung as its head, was being formed and had joined with Sun Yat-sen who had returned from abroad to push the revolution. The Manchu dynasty had fallen, but, because a proper central government, run in democratic style, had not yet been established, the warlords still did much as they pleased. Nevertheless, we needed to return, as there was much to be done while it was day, for the night was coming in China. My mother begged me not to take the two beautiful children back to that horrible place, as she called it. She offered me the lovely home on Gladstone Avenue and $10,000 inheritance if I would only stay home. My father had gone to heaven and only my brother remained. As we said goodbye, telling her that "he that puts his hand to the plough and turns back is not fit for the Kingdom," I knew that I would never see them again on this earth. As I look back now, I would gladly do the same thing, for, in the light of Calvary, there is no real sacrifice.

Appointed Missionaries of the PAOC

"A large crowd of friends and members of the PAOC churches came down to Union Station in Toronto to see us off. We were appointed missionaries now. Stopping in Winnipeg on the way for the Sunday services, I was asked to speak, the pastor being a former classmate at Nyak. Just before going onto the platform, a telegram arrived for me, telling me that my dear brother had succumbed to the flu and had gone to heaven. My heart was broken, but, as I ministered and pled for the millions in China that had never heard, God richly blessed.

"On the journey across the Pacific, Paul developed a severe throat infection. Every member of the family was seasick and could not take care of him, but some of the kind passengers took care of him and he recovered.

Shanghai

"On arriving in Shanghai, we expected to be welcomed by missionaries where we had been invited to minister. However, a lighter came out to meet the boat, and they informed us that, because we were Pentecostal, we would not be welcome. However, a Mrs. Lawyler and her daughter, Beatrice, who were with the Four-Square Mission, hearing of our plight, anxiously sought us out and took us into their home. May the Lord reward them for their many kindnesses to us. We then learned that the area of the Tibetan border was closed to Westerners because of the Civil War going on there and the bandits that ruled the roads, and that it was impossible for us to return to Taojo. While we were waiting and praying for the leading of the Lord, Mother Lawyler, who had just received a new tent and was ready to pitch it on a vacant lot in their neighborhood, invited Ivan to be the evangelist for the meetings. We rented a house near the vacant lot and the meetings began. The Spirit of God moved in mighty power, and many were saved and healed by the hand of God.

"One day, Ivan went out to do the shopping and I was left home alone with the boys. Suddenly two large Russians came to the door leading two Chinese men bound by ropes. They said, "These two men have just killed your husband." It seems that Ivan had been walking on the street when he saw two men in a fight. They faced one another with heavy Chinese hoes raised to strike. Fearing for their lives, in typical fearless fashion, he came between them to stop them. One of the men, angry at the interference, hit Ivan on the head with his heavy hoe, opening a large gash on the scalp. He fell unconscious and lay bleeding to death, as the crowd, in typical fashion, melted away. Providentially, an old white Russian lady was passing by. She had had first aid training, and asked some men to carry Ivan into her little upstairs room nearby. There she was able to stop the flow of blood and save his life. He was taken to the hospital. After getting over the initial shock of hearing that he was dead, I was taken to the hospital as my friend, Mia Jacobson, stayed with the boys. On hearing my footsteps coming into the room, Ivan said, "Don't be frightened. I'll be all right." It was a good thing he warned me, as he was a dreadful sight, so pale and his head wreathed in bandages. That is the kind of man Ivan was — fearless, but filled with God's love and not afraid to risk his life to help his brother, no matter what color his skin.

"Missionary children, too, have experiences that affect their lives. While we were living in Shanghai, a beggar used to roll down the street. He had no arms nor legs, and rolled his torso along the dusty road with such an unearthly cry that the boys stopped their ears and came running in to bury their heads in my skirt when he passed by. One day, when the boys were playing in the vacant lot, they came running to me, crying out that a dog had a little baby. A dog had dug up the body of a little unwanted baby girl. I rushed out and, while I held the dog, the boys went to call for the police to take and bury the dead body of the little unwanted baby girl. Such is the cheapness of life in the Orient, and such are the traumatic experiences of missionaries' children.

The Tsingtao Call

"As we continued in prayer for guidance, the Lord laid upon our hearts the city of Tsingtao, which lay on the coast north of Shanghai, about 24 hours by boat. Even though we knew no one there, Ivan went to spy out the land. He was able to rent living quarters, leaving word for it to be whitewashed, as we would all be coming up the next week to live there. We all set sail again as Abraham, and arrived safely in the beautiful harbor of Tsingtao, which means 'Green Island,' as a little green island lay in the center of the large Kiaochou Bay. No one met us at the dock. The flat which had been rented was still not whitewashed properly, so Ivan left me with the boys on the beach to wait while he hurried the workmen up. As he walked along the street, a well-dressed Chinese gentleman with a big smile stopped him and said, "Are you the one who has come to teach us about the Holy Spirit?" This was Mr. Chou, a druggist in the city. He was a Christian and had been tutoring a Southern Presbyterian missionary, Miss Edith Flower, in Chinese. Miss Flower was one of the first ones to receive the baptism in the Holy spirit in that area. She had prayed with Mr. Chou and he had also received. Together, they prayed that the Lord would send someone to teach them and help to spread the good news. As Mr. Chou prayed, the Lord gave him a vision of the man who would be sent in answer to prayer. As he walked down the street that day, he recognized Ivan as that man. What a wonderful confirmation as to our calling by the Lord to Tsingtao. Meanwhile, on the beach, the boys, being glad to be on terra firma again after a rough voyage, soon began happily throwing stones into the ocean. Donald's aim was rather faulty, however, and he hit Paul on the head, and the blood flowed. It was just a surface cut, and I was soon able to stop the blood with my handkerchief dipped in seawater. When Ivan returned with a big smile on his face, we knew that the Lord was on our side and were ready to face all kinds of trials. The first trial was trying to live in the freshly whitewashed rooms that were still damp. Ivan went back to the docks the next day to get the baggage, and came back saying that he had used almost every penny to get the things through customs. True to form, the Westerner was thought to be wealthy and was bled for as much as possible.

"The next day I took the boys out for a walk to get out of the damp rooms and met a white lady who said, "My husband is the Russian Consul in Tsingtao. We are going on a journey to Russia for a few months and want to rent a room to store some of our things." I told her we had quite a few rooms and could possibly spare one. The lady then paid me in advance for the room. This was God's way of meeting our needs because no mail had come from the Head Office in Toronto, as they had not yet received notice of our whereabouts. There was no air mail in those days.

Small Beginnings

"Mr. Chou was a real godsend to us and helped us to find and rent a small store-front hall downtown on Peking Street where we could begin meetings. He went on to become an ordained elder in the Assembly there, and for many years was used of the Lord in Tsingtao.

"It was my duty to play the small pump organ in the little hall. When the Spirit of God began to move, the little hall became packed. It was now winter and the windows had to be closed to keep out the cold. In North China, the people wear thick-padded garments, and they also like to eat lots of garlic. When the meeting got in full swing and the people were singing and praising the Lord, they began to perspire, and the garlic oozed through the pores of their skin; and one could either wear a gas mask or join them in eating lots of garlic, which is good for the blood, anyway, they tell us.

"In a short time, a missionary doctor's wife, with the Presbyterian church, whose husband had just died, offered us her lovely home for rent. It was on the ground floor of a nice German-built house and had a lovely yard for the boys to play in. When I asked her the rent, my heart sank, as it was far more than we could afford. We were fortunate to get $25.00 a month in our allowance in those days and, even with the exchange, it allowed us very little for rent. She asked, however, how much we were now paying, and agreed to accept the same amount, as she wanted very much to have Westerners in her home. She never returned, and No. 6 Hunan Road became a real haven for us. The cool, deep well in the backyard was ideal for putting watermelons down to cool in the hot summer weather, and we had room to keep a few goats for milk, also. It seemed like paradise compared to life on the borders of Tibet. But we found that there were still many battles yet to fight and victories to be won.

Boarding School

"When the boys were of school age, we were at a loss as to where to send them. We finally sent them to Shanghai to a school run by the Dearborn sisters, friends of Mrs. Lawyler. They were lovely Christian ladies, but, being spinsters, dealt rather harshly with their "little angels." Everything was regimented, even to the time when one should go to the bathroom, pray or eat your porridge. If you failed to obey these rules, or if you were found running up the stairs instead of walking like a little man, you were rewarded by several hard licks with a hair brush, on the place God created for that purpose. Sometimes the punishment was to memorize a whole chapter of the Bible. Paul took it in his stride, and his cute smile enabled him to escape some of the harsher punishments. But Donald got so homesick that he was actually sick. In answer to his fervent prayer, his father had to go and bring them back to Tsingtao. The fact that there was a communist uprising and the Nationalist Party was putting it down with real bullets that were flying everywhere, was just a secondary cause to his childlike faith. The year was 1926.

The Trial Of Our Faith

"On the way back to Tsingtao on the boat, they all slept in a large open area covered with a straw matting, or tatami, Japanese style. Donald, who was still not strong, caught scarlet fever. He had a fever of 104 degrees for 22 days, and the doctor feared for his life and sanity. Finally, an abscess formed behind his eye, and the doctor said he would have to operate and take out the eye and open the abscess, lest it burst and go into the brain. The church had been praying with us for him. But, when they heard this news, they spent all night in fasting and prayer, and that night God's hand was laid upon the lad and, in the morning, the doctor found that a hole had been opened between his eyes by the Great Physician and the pus had all drained out. There was great rejoicing in the church, not to mention in our home.

"The Depression of the early 1930's was in full swing, and sometimes our allowance from Canada failed to arrive, as folks at home were feeling the pinch of the financial depression. I was able to tutor a number of Japanese ladies in English, and this brought in a little extra income, but we had to watch our pennies; and it was wonderful how the Lord made the little money we received stretch out to meet our needs.

"The Lord blessed us with a little girl soon after this, and she was a real joy to me. The loved ones at home sent her such lovely little dresses, and it was a treat to dress the little one up and see how happy the simple things in life made her. God's Spirit was mightily moving in our midst and a strong indigenous church was being built. The Lord was teaching us the principles of an indigenous church in which we must decrease and the

Lord must increase. Little did we dream that, as in the case of John the Baptist, the dark sickle of death would be the means, under God, to bring forth life in the church in China. In 1933 our precious little Betty Jean took diphtheria. Many had been healed in the revival, but the Lord took Betty Jean to Himself. Complications, resulting from scarlet fever and diphtheria, attacked the frail body and her heart gave out. The night before she died she said, "Mama, did you see all those children dressed in white? Oh," she said, "there were so many and I played with them." Because of the conditions at that time, she was not able to go out of the yard and she had very few playmates. But I believe the angels came to play with her that night, preparing her for the trip to her heavenly home, borne on angels' wings. This was a great comfort to us. The loss of his little girl was a great sorrow to Ivan, whose body was suffering from cancer. The following year we took a trip down to Hong Kong where he could have a rest and be examined in the Matilda Hospital, which was free to missionaries, on the beautiful peak overlooking Hong Kong Harbor. The cancer had gone too far, and Ivan did not survive the operation. Burial was mandatory within 24 hours in that tropical climate, so the boys could not be at the funeral. But, again, the Lord was with me to undergird. Donald was in high school in Korea and Paul was in Tsingtao. When the boys received the letters that their beloved Dad had gone to heaven, the Spirit of God spoke to their hearts in their sorrow and called them to take up the cross that Ivan had been compelled to lay down.

"At Ivan's death, Rev. A. G. Ward wrote this poem in his memory:

From foreign lands they sent the word
That he is safe from wind and tide,
And happy on the other side.
But strange that I who loved him well
Should weep as if some woe befell —
Should weep when far from storm and sea
My friend is safe as safe can be."

Chapter V

The Red Dragon Enters

Mao Tse-tung

The year is 1949. High on the T'ien-an-men gate that looks over the great square in the center of Peking, a tall, plump man in a gray uniform waved to the crowd below with a faint smile. The whole square was filled with millions of people singing, "The East is Red. The sun is rising on the horizon of China. Appears the great hero, Mao Tse-tung, Great Saviour of the people." A powerful, masculine voice roared from the loud-speakers, "Ladies and gentlemen, our national anthem." The band struck up again,

> Arise you brave men
> Who do not wish to become slaves;
> Let us use our blood and flesh
> To build a new Great Wall of national defense.

From an insignificant librarian, making 17 Chinese dollars a month (U.S. $5.67), to Dictator of China, able to command the absolute obedience of some one thousand million people, how many people in the world have achieved so much in such a short time? Since the days of the Dragon Emperors, many people had fought for the position he now held, yet only he had succeeded. Why? For one, he had become the high priest of a new, yet old religion in China. Humanism, in the form of Marxism, had at last been able to cast off all the animistic and superstitious traditions of the past and blossom in all its glory. As the millions of red flags are waved, listen to the fine promises this 'saviour' makes to the people: "We will work bravely and industriously to create *our own* civilization and happiness, and will, at the same time, promote world peace and freedom. Our nation will never again be insulted. *We* have stood up." T'ien-an-men means 'Gate of Heavenly Peace,' but heaven is not mentioned or invoked. Man alone becomes his own saviour and Karl Marx his prophet. True, it was a foreign religion, as was

Buddhism centuries ago, and Western, at that. Western institutions had usually been presented to China through missionary influence in the context of Christianity. But, when communism appeared, they turned with relief to a system that claimed to define the whole duty of man without reference to the supernatural. For the Chinese, religions have always been basically humanistic. Here was something they could accept and still retain control of the situation. *Pride* again became the means by which Satan, the great dragon, enslaved men. He, himself, had become forever banished from heaven when, in pride, Lucifer, son of the morning, said, "I will ascend above the heights of the clouds; I will make myself like the Most High" (Isaiah 14:14 NASB).

Let us go back and trace the history of the Red Dragon and how he came to control China and the men he used to do his work.

Mao Tse-tung was born in 1893 to a peasant family in Hunan Province. His father was a shrewd farmer who speculated in the rice market and became prosperous. He was a strict disciplinarian. His son grew to hate him. He also hated his teacher of Confucian Classics. Defiant of authorities, he imaged himself a Chinese Robin Hood, striking against the rich to help the poor. He would have been a rebel without Karl Marx or Lenin. Not only that, but he was greatly disturbed by China's international status. He had a strong sense of nationalism. He was sent to a normal school in Changsha, the capital, but left after only one year to devote his time to patriotic work. He admired Sun Yat-sen. In 1918 he went to Peking where he found a job as assistant librarian with the Peking University. The head of the library was Li Ta-chao, one of the first of the intelligentsia to embrace communism as the solution to China's problems. Under Li's guidance, Mao became Marxist-oriented.

Sun Yat-sen

Sun Yat-sen returned to China in 1923, having raised considerable support for his revolution from overseas Chinese. In 1914 he had met and married one of the Soong sisters, Ch'ing-ling, during his exile in Tokyo. Ch'ing-ling had already studied in Russia, and was very radical in her thinking and influenced Sun greatly. Another factor that pushed Sun toward Russia was the fact that the West turned a deaf ear to his requests for assistance against the imperialistic government and warlords of China, because they, themselves, had many vested interests.

Marxism

Thoroughly disenchanted with the West, China's intellectual leaders began to look elsewhere for a solution to China's problems. Many turned to Russia. The initial attraction to Marxism was not because of any inherent value the Chinese may have seen in Marxist theory, for they, being called the Jews of the Orient, have always thrived on private enterprise. Their fine work ethic and industriousness are well known. But it was a positive response to the victory of the Russian Revolution in 1917. Chinese nationalists, who had often compared China's situation to that of Tzarist Russia, looked to Marxism as a possible guide for revolutionary success. The claims to scientific truth of the Marxist theory also appealed to many Chinese who had virtually made a god of what they called 'Mr. Science.'

Although a Western theory, Marxism proved more acceptable to sensitive Chinese nationalists than other alien ideas because it condemned not only the Chinese traditions but those of the West as well, and it was humanistic. More immediately enticing was the Karakhan proposal which reached China in March 1920, promising that the new Soviet government would give up former Russian rights in China. It was an attractive package to nationalists, like Li Ta-Chao, the first influential convert to Marxism, and his young library assistant at Peking National University, Mao Tse-tung.

Books that bolstered the humanistic philosophy were rapidly also being translated into Chinese, such as the work of Charles Darwin on "The Origin of Species" and Huxley's "Evolution & Ethics." These had a great influence on the already humanistically-oriented minds of China's intelligentsia and the students, many of whom had studied in Europe in an age when higher criticism was the fad and no decent scholar would dare to proclaim his faith in the Bible as the infallible Word of God for fear of being laughed at by the intelligentsia.

May 4 Movement

Just 30 years before Mao delivered his famous "We have stood up" speech in T'ien-an-men Square on May 4, 1919, a group of students gathered at the same site and demonstrated against the government's intention of signing the Versailles Treaty, which would give Kiaochou Bay in Shangtung to Japan, and shouted, "Give us back Tsingtao." Thirty-two students were arrested. One of these students was *Chou En Lai*. They called the day China signed the "21 demands" from Japan, "China's day of humiliation." The Versailles Treaty was later reversed at the Washington Conference in 1921, and the protests of the students, some of whom had studied in the U.S., had been heard. China would no longer lease her territory, with the exception of Hong Kong, to foreign nations. An open door policy for all nations was reiterated. Foreign post offices in China were abolished, and tariff and extraterritoriality questions were discussed. The students had successfully stopped China from signing the Versailles Treaty and won back Tsingtao, and for the next 30 years, the students claimed to be the guardians of the nation's spirit, sometimes completely disregarding discipline. The May 4 Movement, as it was called, had been inspired by the individualism and free-thinking of the West, learned in mission schools. But, being directed against warlordism and imperialism, it had to be anti-Western, for, the Western powers, as we have mentioned, were committed to the support of some warlords and the imperialism that brought special privileges to them. So the May 4 Movement eventually turned toward the left and became the radical wing of the Kuomintang Party. The West was helping to suppress the student agitation, but Moscow renounced all its special rights and enthusiastically applauded the May 4 Movement.

In 1921 the first meeting of the Communist Party took place in Shanghai in a little back room. Mao was present and Sun Yat-sen was elected Secretary General in absentia. Gregory Voitinsky had been sent from Russia to organize the Chinese Communist Party. At the first there were only 50 members. But by 1923, when Sun Yat-sen returned from abroad, there were 432 members. Michael Borodin, the most influential of all the Soviet advisers, was sent to China to help them draw up a constitution for the Kuomintang Party.

Thus, Sun Yat-sen's revolution now had the backing of the students and the friendship of Russia which included financial and military aid. Also, Borodin persuaded Sun that he could add the principles of the Soviets to the Kuomintang program without disloyalty to his ideals.

Chiang Kai-shek

The Russians helped to establish a Military Academy in Shanghai called The Whangpoa Military Academy. A young officer, Chiang Kai-shek, was made commandant and Chou En-lai was made his deputy and political commissar. After his arrest in Peking at the May 4 incident, Chou went to France as a work student. But neither work nor study were his primary interests. He helped form a branch of the Chinese Communist Party in France. In 1924 when communists, both Russian and Chinese, were admitted to the Kuomintang party on condition that they adopt the principles of the Kuomintang, Chou returned to China. But communist members added their own slogans of communism, anti-capitalism, anti-imperialism and anti-Christianity. These new doctrines proved to be just the seed to sprout in the rich loam of growing nationalism. It was into this mixture of democracy, socialism and communism that there arose one force that seemed to offer China hope without violent overthrow and purges, and that was *Christianity*. After long having established schools and hospitals and having preached the life-transforming gospel, the time had arrived for its trial of fire.

In the fall of 1927 Chiang was converted to Christianity as a Methodist, and late in that year he married Soong Mei-ling, a beautiful, talented young woman who came from a business-man's family and had been educated in the U.S. The mother of Mei-ling was a very devout Pentecostal Christian. Mei-ling was the sister of Ch'ing-ling who had married Sun Yat-sen. Although Ch'ing-ling had also received some education in the U.S., she had been influenced by Russian friends and never professed a faith in God. The two girls had a great influence on their husbands, each in the opposite direction. If Ch'ing-ling had yielded her life to Christ, how different the history of China could have become. The husband may be the head of the family, but often it is the wife who is the neck that turns the head. If Sun Yat-sen, who was also a Christian, had had the same spiritual support from his wife as Chiang Kai-shek, there might never have been a split in the party, one to the right and one to the left, that eventually brought on a civil war. Chiang Kai-shek could have spent all his energy in fighting corruption in the government and, later on, fighting the Japanese instead of having to use all his energy trying to suppress the members of his party who had come under the strong influence of Russia and atheistic communism.

In 1925 Sun Yat-sen died and the party came under Chiang Kai-shek's leadership. The left wing of the party sacked Hankow, and six missionaries were killed. This was done to discredit the party and caused a split. The three peoples' principles, formed by Sun Yat-sen, were:

1. Nationalism — a united China;
2. Democratic authority — establishing a republic; and,
3. Social reforms — land ownership by the common man.

The Left Wing complained that Chiang had not followed the third principle, and Madam Sun, denouncing the party for giving up this principle, went to Moscow. In hindsight, it now seems that Chiang's more moderate policy of reducing the rent charged by landlords, rather than liquidating the land-owners and giving their land to the so-called common men who, in turn, became serfs working for the state, may have worked better. But Chiang's policy never was given a fair chance.

The Failure of the Kuomintang

At first, the Kuomintang, under Chiang Kai-shek, did a good job of stabilizing the economy. Under T. V. Soong, the Foreign Minister, who was a brother of the famous Soong sisters, they were very scrupulous in meeting their foreign debts. In 1931, when the country was first attacked by Japan and a great flood of the Yangtze River destroyed 12 million homes, they still made their payments. However, the Western powers still would not agree to the relinquishment of extraterritoriality and the giving up of concessions and settlements, which Russia had done some years before. A considerable program of road building, financed by foreign loans, was quite successful, but foreign trade diminished. By the time the Japanese invaded China, and they had to put all their efforts into defense, the nationalists' efforts at rebuilding the nation and earning popular support had already been lost. As a republic, run on rather democratic lines, there was too much corruption by local officials and not a strong enough central government that demanded obedience, such as a totalitarian government could demand. Besides defending the nation from Japan, they spent much time and money in fighting the communists who had infiltrated the northern portion of the land.

China's three great problems remained unsolved: (1) famine; (2) transportation (air mail and passenger service); (3) education (many mission schools closed). Four thousand missionaries left

China and, by 1928, over one-half had left and handed over the work to the Chinese brethren as a result of the Civil War. The greater the pressures from Japan and the communists, the greater the development of the indigenous movements in Chinese churches.

In 1929, Japan withdrew all forces from Shangtung, but it was not until 1930 that Chiang was able to gain the support of warlords in the north, Feng and Yen, and, in 1931, in Peking, adopt a provisional constitution. The third principle of land reform was as yet not implemented, and the Communist Party, although expelled from the Kuomintang in 1927, with many fair promises gained the support of the farmers, who comprise a great portion of the population.

The Kuomintang built 2,000 miles of dykes in 1931 and re-formed the currency. In the same year a Chinese Soviet Republic was formally established, with Mao Tse-tung as President. The soviets called for joint efforts against the Japanese. Chiang tried to destroy the Red Army in 1934, but the famous "Long March" saved them. Ninety thousand men started out and about 45,000 arrived in Shensi to set up their headquarters. Chiang still hoped for peace with Japan so they could together wipe out the Reds. Chiang had ordered the Manchurian Army to fight the Reds, but when they refused, in December 1936 he flew up to Sian to enforce his command and was kidnapped by the army there and held for 14 days. He found that the army had been infiltrated by the Reds. This revolt, many feel, triggered the formal declaration of war with Japan. Chou En-lai rushed to Sian to help, and when Chiang agreed to stop the Civil War and release political prisoners, Chiang was released. All China rejoiced, and Chiang was a great national hero for a season. The Soviet Republic of China now became the bordering District of Shensi, Kansu and Ningsia, and the Red Army became the Eighth Route Army of the National Army of China.

Japan Attacks

The severance of Manchuria from China, in the "Manchurian incident," did not satisfy the expansion-hungry Japanese.

In the spring of 1937, Chou En-lai held a series of discussions with his former commander of the Whampao Academy, and the second period of cooperation between the Kuomintang and the communists began; but, before the agreement was even completed, Japan struck at the Marco Polo Bridge in Peking and formal war was declared against Japan.

By the end of 1939, two years after the outbreak of hostilities, Japan had conquered the northeastern one-third of the country, the most populous and productive region in China. In September of that year, World War II began, and Japan had other enemies. After Pearl Harbor, China, which was in a very drained situation financially, no longer fought alone. Roosevelt ordered the delivery of military equipment and a gift of $500 million, which helped to stabilize the runaway inflation. General Stilwell of the United States, who could not seem to tolerate Chiang, began to arm all the Chinese, including the communists. Chiang, being more of a statesman than a soldier, saw the danger and had Stilwell dismissed.

The Russian Bear Hug

The U.S. and Great Britain concluded treaties with China in January of 1943, providing relinquishment of extraterritorial rights. Thus, for the first time in 100 years, the Chinese courts had jurisdiction over British and American citizens in China, and the remaining concessions were returned to China.

However, this joy was short-lived as, in February 1945, Roosevelt, Churchill and Stalin at Yalta decided to give the Soviet Russians jurisdiction over Manchuria, supposedly with China retaining full sovereignty. This was done without China's knowledge. Following the dropping of the first atomic bomb on Hiroshima on August 6, the Soviet army, which had not helped against Japan up to that time, entered the war by marching into Manchuria. The Japanese army offered little resistance and the invaders took over Manchuria. After Japan's surrender on August 21, the Russians were in a good position to help their comrades, the Chinese communists.

Seventy thousand U.S. soldiers remained in China after the war, and the U.S. became very unpopular. In 1946, a student in Peking accused a G.I. of rape which started a violent reaction across the land.

Chiang promised that the Red Army would be wiped out in six months. He had four million men; the Reds had only one million. He lost.

Swallowed by the Red Dragon

What tipped the balance in favor of the communists was their success in convincing the peasants that they could better themselves if they followed them. They promised to do better in the fields of social justice and economic welfare. In the countryside, the most serious problem had been, and still was, the land problem. The communists resolved it by liquidating landlords and dividing the expropriated land among the peasants who, of course, later were forced to work for the state, but they did not know it at that time. This was not a true solution because the Chinese problem was essentially a problem of shortage rather than of distribution. For the time being, however, their program appeased the peasants who fought their wars, and fought so well that they conquered the Nationalist Army. Deserters from the Nationalist Army swelled the Red Army and, by 1949, they had chased Chiang out of the mainland to Taiwan.

The weakness of the nationalist government was its inability to think in social terms in its anti-communist crusade. It regarded communism as a military issue which, unfortunately, it was not. If it were, it would have been eliminated a long time ago. The red dragon had seemingly conquered by appealing to the selfish needs of the people. Mao was their god and the little red book, the sayings of Mao, their Bible. Nothing was impossible, they were told, if only one used the thoughts of Mao. The people were promised freedom of speech, freedom of the press, freedom of assembly, freedom of association, freedom of procession and freedom of demonstration. But these freedoms, under the 1975 constitution, are conditioned by the fact that all citizens must support the Chinese Communist Party leadership at all times and without reservation. In other words, a Chinese can exercise these freedoms to praise or support the C.C.P. leaders or the policies and programs they have adopted, but they cannot criticize or oppose them. This so-called "utopia" is called the dictatorship of the C.C.P. leadership. In order to do this, they had to build a leader larger than life. No emperor in China's long past had been built up to such a superhuman proportion as Mao.

Party members have been installed as cadres in China and are now enjoying special privileges. Some have become lazy and corrupt and, as is only human, very selfish, and the needs of the common man are forgotten. The old revolutionaries that have held sway in the land for some 30 years are being blamed with the failure of the cultural revolution and will, no doubt, be purged.

Starting slowly at first with a number of good non-communist reforms to gain the confidence of the people and even some of the missionaries, they were soon firmly in the saddle. When once in power the fireworks began. Land-owners were executed. Christians, even of indigenous churches, were imprisoned and martyred. There have been at least 10 purges of party members during the 30 years. The **1980 Guinness Book of Records** states that, since 1949, when the communists took over, 63,787,000 people have been liquidated by the party in China.[12] The red dragon has become drenched in human blood.

The communists have been able to carry out many improvements in the land. Being a totalitarian state, they have been able to rule with an iron hand and accomplish a number of things that a more democratic government could not do. This is nothing new for China. For instance, the Great Wall, stretching for thousands of miles over the rough, mountainous terrain of North China, was built by slave labor under such a totalitarian government. But the strong work ethic of the Chinese people has sadly suffered as a result. One sees many people standing around idle — so uncharacteristic of the Chinese people. It seems that, with so many purges and changes, the people do not know what or who to believe and have lost heart. I am sure that, with a more benevolent government and more private enterprise, the hardworking, ingenius people of China could improve their country to a much greater extent than during the past 32 years.

How did the church survive that kind of treatment? There is only one way to combat this red dragon who breathes fire and brimstone and death, and that is with the mighty infilling of the Holy Ghost and fire with which John the Baptist promised Jesus would baptize His church. Let us examine the *revival* that enabled the church to fight fire with fire and come out more than conquerors.

Chapter VI

Fighting Fire With Holy Ghost Fire

Korea

The fire of the Holy Ghost that would purge the church would also give it the power to overcome the dragon and establish the church in China. This was the philosophy that drove the church to its knees at the beginning of this century. The missionaries in Korea decided to meet every day at the noon hour until the Lord revived His church in that land. After a month of prayer, someone suggested that they give it up and get back to practical work. But the majority decided that, instead of discontinuing the prayer meetings, they would give more time to prayer, not less. With that in view, they changed the hour from noon to four o'clock in the afternoon so they could pray until supper time or longer, if they wished. They kept it up until, at last, after months of waiting, the answer came. And it has been a praying church every since. The result has been a church that outlasted the Japanese occupation in 1910 and the communist war, and is now growing faster than the population.

Goforth

In China both missionaries and nationals met each day for prayer, and the Holy Spirit began to melt the hearts of His people and purge sin from their ranks. Jonathan Goforth declared:

> All unconfessed sin in the believer, of whatever kind, mars the redemptive work of Christ. The most piercing cries that I have ever heard have come from Chinese Christians when the Holy Spirit made plain to them that their sin had crucified the Son of God afresh. The filth and blood-guiltiness of the church can only be swept away by the spirit of judgment and burning.[13]

The missionaries testified to the mighty convicting power of God:

A power has come into the church we cannot control, if we would. It is a miracle for stolid, self-righteous John Chinaman to go out of his way to confess to sins that no torture of the Yamen could force from him, for a Chinese to demean himself, to crave, weeping, the prayers of his fellow believers is beyond all human explanation.[14]

But this is just what the church needed.

Shangtung Revival

The revival in Shangtung, a little later on in the century, began in the same way. I remember early morning prayer meetings in a large Baptist Church in Tsingtao when Christians of all denominations gathered to seek the face of the Lord for revival. The Lord showed them a dark cloud about to cover the land. This prophecy was fulfilled in the Japanese invasion and later in the communist take-over. God wanted a glorious church without spot or wrinkle to stand in that hour against the forces of the dragon, that men might see the reality of what it means to be a child of God. Many had joined the church for pragmatic reasons, because it seemed a good way to prosper materially, but they had never truly repented of sin and made Jesus Lord of their lives. This was a purging time for the church. For example, one church elder stood up and confessed he had wronged one of the widows who had called him to her deathbed. Before dying, she had given him a goodly sum of money and asked him to take care of her children and other needs. He confessed he had done this with part of the money, but had kept part of it, invested it, and had become prosperous, much like Ananias and Sapphira in the early church. In agony of soul and with great sobs of repentance, the elder confessed his sin, asked forgiveness of the people, and asked that they pray that God would forgive him also. Later he returned with the money he had taken, with the interest made on it, and cast it from him on the altar as if it had been a fiery serpent. The people embraced him, comforted him, and, one by one, rose to confess their sins and make restitution as the fear of God fell upon the congregation.

Such was the moving of God's Spirit in 1929 when Ivan and Frances Kauffman returned from their furlough in Canada. Ivan Kauffman wrote in the August, 1931 issue of **The Pentecostal Testimony**:

When the revival struck this city, not one of the churches was really in a position to recognize it or to openly accept it. Finally, in desperation, these hungry people were driven to the formerly despised Pentecostal church, there to find, to their great relief, not only a haven of rest, but a place where, unhindered, they were permitted to seek God to their heart's content, not only for salvation, but for the gracious outpouring of the Holy Spirit in real Pentecostal power. There is a daily prayer meeting from 5:30 a.m. to 7:00 a.m., then a daily Bible study at 9:00 a.m. In every meeting there are not less than six people confessing their sins and oftentimes as many as ten to fifteen. I don't believe I have ever heard such crying and weeping before the Lord or confessions of such awful sins. One of the remarkable features is that at confession many are healed of all kinds of sicknesses.[15]

He also wrote:

There are deeply spiritual quickenings of Pentecostal power and blessing through this Province in the Baptist and Presbyterian missions, as well as our own, such as, a year ago, would have been considered impossible. Even in our church, a few years ago, it would have been impossible for the pastor to ask the people to kneel and pray. Now they want no pads for their knees, but gladly kneel on the cold and, not any too clean, cement with their lovely silk gowns. It seems they cannot humble themselves enough. Now they all pray together with a tremendous volume of voices ascending to the Throne of Grace three or four times every meeting.

Among those that have been baptized in the Spirit are quite a few missionaries in many of the large denominations, as well as many national workers. All praise to our adorable Lord.[16]

Ivan Kauffman was able to rent a large hall, seating some 1,000 people, for their meeting place. In this hall the presence of the Lord was so real that any unsaved man coming in immediately felt tears come to his eyes as conviction of sin settled down on him. Little children fell prostrate under the power of God's Spirit and spoke, in beautiful unaccented English, the praises of God, even though they had never spoken English before. The healing power of God was manifest mightily as there were services every night. Rev. George Kelley, a missionary from Canton, was invited to come up for special meetings, teaching on the Holy Spirit. He spoke in Cantonese and Mary Liang interpreted into Mandarin. But many times no one dared to stand up to speak, as the presence of God caused all present to fall on their faces before God and weep. Strong men, even church elders and leaders, stood to confess sins. The purifying, purging fire of the Holy Spirit swept through the church as a whole. Presbyterian, Baptist, Anglican, Lutheran and Assembly of God all came under the purging fire of the Spirit of God. Church members and even leaders in the church found out that they had never been truly born again into a living relationship with Christ.

God had led Ivan Kauffman to this strategic area in 1923 when a small work began; but now, it was not just a local church, it was a move of God's Spirit over all that area. Tsingtao was a beautiful city, and many of the large brick and stucco houses and business places had been built by the Germans before the First World War. They reflected the past when the West had exploited China and the missionary got the name of "imperialist." All this was being wiped out in a short time by the moving of the Holy Spirit, and unity and love between national and missionary was beautiful to see. The Lord was preparing His Church for a sifting time to come under the Japanese and later under the communists.

"When the Enemy Cometh in as a Flood"

As is often the case while China was going through political turmoil, God's Spirit, in answer to a heart-felt cry from His people, began to send the fire of purging and reviving to His Church. Let the church settle down and become too comfortable and respectable, and it will be in danger of drying up spiritually. When the judgements of God are in the land, only then do the people learn righteousness, it seems. Similar moves of the Spirit of God in other parts of China, such as that under the ministry of John Sung and the Bethel Bands with Andrew Gih, stirred the church in China in the days of political upheaval and war. But none had a greater impact on the church in China than the so-called Shangtung Revival of the early 1930's. Many of the strong leaders of the church, who were to lead the church under God into the future days of testing and strife, met God during the days of revival in North China, and Ivan Kauffman was one of the weak persons that God used to confound the mighty. Much division and bigotry was swept away, and the love of God was shed abroad by the Holy Spirit as they humbled themselves before the cross.

The Indigenous Church

This was the time when the church began to become indigenous, and many indigenous church groups, such as the "True Jesus Church" and "The Jesus Family," came into being. Making the church indigenous became an obsession with many of the missionaries, and they sought by methods of man rather than through prayer and the moving of the Holy Spirit to produce a so-called indigenous church. Even the communists, using the so-called "Three-Self Movement," involved so-called indigenous church methods to further their cause. Its motivation cannot be nationalism or a spirit of independence or pride. The true church of Jesus Christ, that becomes a part of the culture and family life of the people, must be born of the Spirit of God, who, alone, makes God's Word apply to all cultures.

I would like to quote again from Dr. Nelson Bell, Billy Graham's father-in-law, who was a missionary in China for many years, because I believe he recognized and admitted the mistakes we have made in trying to create an indigenous church in China by our so-called New Testament methods without the New Testament dynamic of the Holy Spirit. He said, some years ago,

> I feel now, however, that we have permitted the pendulum to swing too far. We are actually subsidizing national churches in areas where they should be standing on their own feet. We are giving precedence to national church leaders in a way which often frustrates our missionaries and, at the same time, downgrades them in the eyes of those with whom they work. We have taken to ourselves decisions regarding national churches without, in my judgment, sufficient advice from our own missionaries. The effect of this precipitate shift in policy is to cause the national churches to look to us primarily for money, and our missionaries are only being sent out to work under national churches. This is a far cry from the New Testament church, and is actually inter-church aid, not foreign mission work. I am convinced that I have contributed to our going too far in this, and that we are harming and holding back national churches rather than advancing the cause of Christ as we had hoped.[17]

Indeed, this is food for thought, even today!

The Refining Fires of Persecution

The Lord has a way of causing even our mistakes, made out of ignorance rather than malice, to be rectified. In China, under the communist takeover, missionaries had to leave, and this was the equalizer that rectified many of those mistakes. Of course, financial dependence on western churches was cut off, and they had to trust God for their financial needs or die. The truly indigenous groups, such as "The Jesus Family," which had no connection with the west, continued on and, because of their communal nature, were difficult to stamp out. The communists who, at first, declared there would be religious liberty, had to take off the kid gloves and reveal the true nature of their entirely humanistic, anti-God movement. The sheep and goats were clearly divided. The Pseudo-Indigenous Church group, called the "Three-Self Movement," which was directed by the government, not only banned churches with connections with the West, but also the truly Chinese indigenous churches, such as the "Little Flock" and "The True Jesus Church," who sought first the Kingdom of God.

For instance, in the Shanghai dog racing stadium, between May and August of 1951, 63 big accusation rallies were held. All churches were required to attend and were forced to propagandize in line with the ideology of the state. Chou En-lai said, "Cooperation with the state's common program of reform was the price of religious freedom,"[18] and missionaries were called imperialists and were forced to leave China.

Watchman Nee was accused by his own church members that had been brought under the control of the state Three-Self Movement. They accused him of frequenting brothels and being an indiscriminate womanizer. They said he had confessed to seducing over a hundred women, both Chinese and foreign, but no evidence was produced. This brother was imprisoned with turncoats who, for their own profit, offered to turn state's witness. Finally, he was put under house arrest because of his age and died, rather than cooperate with their schemes to discredit the Church of Jesus Christ and the missionaries.

Wang Ming Tao, an independent preacher who neither served no headed an organization, but was respected nationally as a leader of true Christians, could not be accused along this line. So, political insinuations were found from his writings. A few of his former supporters were found ready to put themselves in the party's favor by accusing him of treasonable intent. He was imprisoned and forced to confess. Later he denied the confession and tried to refute it.

Although he is now blind he is still under house arrest. He was offered freedom to leave China if he would sign a statement that would link the church with the imperialists and follow the line of the Three-Self Movement, but he refused.

These are the experiences of just two prominent leaders of the church. Thousands, like them, suffered imprisonment and death. Some who were able were scattered abroad, like Elders Chou and Chin, who were druggists and were able to escape to Taiwan where they became elders in the Assembly of God church there. Many others were displaced into other areas of China, as were the early church members, preaching the gospel as they went. Pastor Hsia, Pastor Shung and Elder Peter Chang, to name just a few, were never heard from again, and, no doubt, sealed their testimony with their blood. These were the men who were left in Tsingtao to lead the church when Bro. Clare Scratch, who took Ivan Kauffman's place, left.

Thus, we see that if it had not been for the revival that purged the church and prepared it by enduing it with power, it could have been completely wiped out by this kind of suppression. The church had not only to survive the departure of all missionaries and the cutting off of all funds from abroad, but the moral challenge of communism. The communists had a deep sense of dedication, calling forth such discipline and self-sacrifice as to shame the Christians who had considered themselves the only ones in China willing to make sacrifices for their beliefs. The fourth shock was daily living under the authority of a hostile government, such as the early church Christians in the Roman Empire. They became second-class citizens; their children could not get into a decent school; their young people could not get a job. The communists persuaded many to abandon a heavenly paradise for an earthly one. Today, the communists have accomplished many of their goals, but it has been at the price of people's freedom. The people in China are not only denied the freedom of speech, but also, most regrettably, the freedom of silence — a freedom precious to all those who, being a-political, want to be left alone. It may be true that, before the communist takeover, they did not have political freedom, but today the people do not have the civil liberties they had before, such as the liberty of choosing one's own occupation and residence. Today a Chinese cannot move from one occupation to another or one place to another without Communist Party approval. The so-called "heaven on earth" has been so long in coming that many are becoming disillusioned and have lost faith in communism. They have also lost faith in their old traditional humanistic religions and are living in a spiritual vacuum, ready for the gospel that will truly satisfy their souls from time to eternity.

Their humanistic religions teach of sin and forgiveness, but it comes very lightly. It is forgiven on easy terms, and, to them, it is safer to offend God than men. Only a holy, righteous God of love knows the full destructive power of sin and is able and willing to pay the awful price of our redemption. When we plead the saving power of the blood of Christ, demons flee and we become forever the bondslaves of His love. To believe yourself forgiven while you love the sin that nailed Jesus to the cross and continue to live in the practice of it, is to believe a lie, a monstrous lie. True forgiveness is the work of the Holy Spirit, and produces not only justification, but obedience and a spontaneous desire to be like the One who has given us forgiveness. If God's didn't spare His only begotten Son when He took our sins upon Himself, how shall He spare those who prefer their sins to their Saviour? Only a true Holy Spirit revival in the church will produce the kind of new man that will turn the world right side up again.

"The result of this revival has been the raising up of a wonderful indigenous church that has practically belted the land of China. It has raced over the great plains of North China, gone into the mountains of the West, and it has gone across the Strait into the Island of Formosa (Taiwan), and, today, it has spread abroad. By shutting down the churches and imprisoning the leaders, the communists have taken the fire and they have scattered it, and now they have thousands of fires to contend with. John the Baptist foretold that Jesus would baptize His Church with the Holy Ghost and fire. We believe that this mighty fire is the only way to bring the gospel to every nation as a witness and bring back the King of Kings and the defeat of the dragon."[19]

Chapter VII

Epilogue

My brother, Paul, and I went back to Tsingtao recently to relive some of our childhood experiences. We were also anxious to feel the pulse of the people of China who have been going through perhaps the greatest, most devastating, revolution of all time. We wanted to know if the concerted effort to stamp out the Church of Jesus Christ in China had been successful, and what the response of the young people, born since the revolution, was to the gospel.

The Underground Church

First, we found the church (ecclesia) intact but greatly changed in form. Many of the denominational divisions were gone. Although many of the local groups, who met regularly for prayer and Bible study, are charismatic in practice, they do not carry the Pentecostal handle. They just call themselves Christians. Under the guise of the Three-Self Movement, the government has given back some of the church buildings to the Christian groups, and some of the pastors of these churches, who are truly born from above, are allowed to preach the Word of God there, but they must, of course, put the party first. For this reason there is still considerable fear on behalf of the majority of Christians that the government may change its lenient policy, as it has done so many times before. Therefore, I would say that the majority of the true church still meet in house churches. This so-called underground church (although because of the neighborhood spy system in China it is impossible to hide) meets in homes or isolated places where officials are more sympathetic, and there are more and more cadres being reached with the gospel and turning to Christ. The government is even printing a limited number of Bibles, but, in order to buy one, one must register with the government and would, no doubt, be subject to sanctions, should the government policy change again. The newly opened church buildings are packed well before service time with hungry people of all ages who are so hungry for Christian fellowship and the preaching of the Word that they are willing to risk such government policy change. It is now possible to say that the church in China has grown almost ten-fold since the communist takeover in 1949.

A Spiritual Vacuum

As we met the man on the street, we found that there was an openness toward the gospel and the message of Jesus' love on the cross, that I had never seen before. A young guide said, "We have been taught by our government that science and technology will solve all our problems. But you, in the west, have developed far ahead of us in these fields and it hasn't solved your problems." As I witnessed to him of the living God who created us in His own image, and the fact that man will never be satisfied until he finds the way to come to this God and receive forgiveness for his rebellion and begins to follow the purpose for which God created him in the first place, he, like so many we met, opened his heart and eagerly received the Word of God.

A God With Clay Feet

As Mao Tse-tung grew more feeble, the radicals under Chiang Ch'ing, Mao's wife, were growing stronger, especially after the death of Chou En-lai. However, before they were able to push aside Hua Guo-fang, Mao died. At Mao's death on September 6, 1976, the radical left was confronted with a 'now or never' situation, and moved quickly to gain power. The moderates had no choice but to back Hua and the leaders of the regular army who did their part in keeping the People's Militia in their proper place. The radicals went so far, some say, as to forge Mao's will to achieve their purpose. On October 6, 1976, Chiang Ch'ing, Chang Ch'un-chiao, Wang Hung-jen and Yao Wen-yuan, referred to as the 'Gang of Four,' were arrested, thus averting a major Civil War. Real power then rested with Teng Hsiao-ping. Although just a third-ranking party member, he had the full support of the army, in the government and among the C.C.P. rank and file. For a man who had been twice purged by Mao and Chiang Ch'ing as a capitalist roader, a rightist deviationist, a demon and a freak, this power reversal could not have been more dramatic and complete. Their god, Mao, was found to have clay feet and, at the trial of the Gang of Four, Mao was pulled down from his pedestal. Today, Mao's little red book, we found, had almost completely vanished from China, and the millions of youth who read it as their Bible, no longer do. But, "the Word of the Lord endures forever."

The door to the West has been opened again, and pragmatism has won over ideology, as China has virtually admitted to the failure of Marxism to meet the needs of the people of China. The youth of China are now eager to learn English and are open for what a new era of relationship with the west may offer them. This time, let us not go into China to re-establish mission stations. Let us not try to exploit the opening door in order to raise money to build our western 'Churchianity.' Remember that this spiritual vacuum in the hearts of the youth of China is neutral. It will suck in the good and the bad. Therefore, let us not export our rebellion against authority, our drugs and drunkenness, our promiscuity, our violence and sex, or our obsession with the occult and the horoscope. With the love of Christ, which is always unselfish, let us help the Chinese church, not with money that would make them dependent on us, but with prayer and all that would encourage them, such as Bibles and training of Chinese youth; being careful not to shape them into our mold or indoctrinate them in the very selfish, success-oriented mind-set of Western Christianity. Under the mighty hand of God, the church in China has come a long way in reproducing the New Testament Church. Let us not drag it down to our level. A great door and effectual is opening unto us, but let us not make the same mistakes as in the past.

As we went back to Tsingtao, we found the old home on #6 Hunan Road where we had lived as boys. There were now five families living where we had lived, in very crowded conditions. Several families also lived in the basement where we had stored coal and wood for heating in the winter. But they were very kind and received us in for a cup of tea and a chat. We felt restrained in trying to find Christians who may have remembered us and the days of revival in the 1930's, lest we bring unneeded attention to bear upon them. However, when we returned to Hong Kong, where I had been teaching in Ecclesia Bible Institute and where my brother, Paul, has been preparing a new Bible in the modern script for China in his "Asian Outreach" office, we met a Chinese friend. He was able to visit Tsingtao some time later and he brought back some very interesting news. He said that he had been able to contact the Christians there.

65

Being a Chinese, he was free to go about without a guide who is always a party member. The Christians said they had known when we arrived in Tsingtao, where we had gone, such as to visit the grave of our sister, Betty Jean (all the gravestones, however, had been removed during the Cultural Revolution), and even what we had said. Many of them, no doubt, would have forgotten Ivan Kauffman, and that is the way he would have wanted it. Another brother told us there were some 30 house churches within a small radius in Tsingtao. But they knew Jesus Christ, and that's all that really mattered. We have but to plant the seed of the gospel and water it with the Word of God. As we pray, the Lord will nurture it with the outpouring of His latter rain; and it will continue to reproduce new men, born from above, generation after generation in any culture and in any political clime. That is why Jesus said, "I will build My church (we are but His fellow-laborers; He is the boss); and the gates of hell shall not prevail against it (Matthew 16:18).

A Frustrated Dragon

How frustrated the dragon must be as he sees the church of Jesus Christ in China, not only growing, but, because it meets in homes, becoming a force among the common people; an indigenous church in the true sense. This force is making new men — something Mao failed to do. In order to produce this kind of a church in China, God allowed the communists to literally dismantle the structured church with its system of hierarchy and its Western-style 'churchianity.' Saltshakers with gothic windows and elevated pulpits were taken over by an anti-Christ government. The salt began to be shaken out into the world where it alone could do its saving, healing and preserving work. The church got back to the early Biblical, New Testament church concept of every member in the body of Christ being the temple of God; and, "where two or three are gathered in Jesus' Name," the church in its purest form existed. I am glad that the dragon is not omniscient, nor infallible. He made the same mistake with the early church and, before Satan was able to lure the church into becoming an organization with political overtones instead of a living organism, it had reached the whole, then-known, world for Christ.

The Dragon's Last Fight

In China, Satan is again waking up to the fact that his strong-armed tactics are not working and is changing them again. The

Religious Affairs Department has declared that only designated clergy are authorized to speak or preach the Word of God, thus trying to counteract the mighty power of the ordinary believer, filled with the Holy Ghost, going everywhere, preaching the gospel, healing the sick and casting out the demons. They have also tried to outlaw the house churches, and, through the Three-Self Movement, are trying to force Christians to again confine their worship to formal church buildings only. More fierce persecution may follow for the house churches.

But the church that has gone through the fiery furnace and met the Son of Man is no longer afraid of the enemy. They know that 'Sheung Di,' or the Emperor of Heaven, is soon sending His Son, Jesus Christ, back to earth again, and this time the old serpent will be bound and cast into the bottomless pit. Then they, who have been faithful even unto death, will reign with Christ on earth a thousand years. After that the dragon will be let loose again for a short while to test the nations. For even God, though omnipotent, cannot produce a saint instantaneously. Character is developed through testing, not by an instant miracle. Man, created in the image of God with a free will, must be allowed to make a decision. This requires a choice; Satan provides that alternative or choice. Unlike Adam in the garden, man today has a lot more going for him. Through Jesus, the Son of God, who took upon Him our flesh and became sin for us on the cross, defeating Satan on his own ground and rising victorious from the dead, we now have an advocate who stands with us in the battle. We can overcome Satan by the Blood of the Lamb and by the Word of God made active to us personally by the Holy Spirit.

It hardly seems possible but, even after living for a thousand years under the Theocracy of Christ, in a perfect environment without war or cruelty, when the dragon once again offers to man freedom from God, many will follow the dragon rather than submit to the Lordship of Christ; thus proving that it is not the system of government that is wrong, nor the environment, but the unregenerate heart of man that must be changed before all the problems that plague the world can be solved.

When Jesus, the Prince of Peace, was born into our world, the angels sang "Peace on earth, to men of good will." God knows that the world will never have true peace until men accept the Prince of Peace as their Lord, and become men of good will. Therefore, everyone who rejects this Prince must be exiled to a place prepared for the dragon and his angels, who led in the rebellion against God. This place is called the 'Lake of Fire,' because, among other reasons, to be separated from God's love for eternity is the most horrible torture one could imagine. Then the world will thenceforth have no more trouble with the dragon throughout the endless ages of peace.

However, until that day we are in a battle, not against any political party, ideology or leader on earth, but against the spiritual forces of wickedness in the heavenly places. We hold no grudge and have no bitterness in our hearts against those who have persecuted the Church and even shed the blood of the martyrs, for, it has really become the seed of the Church. But for God's grace manifested to us, we might have been in their shoes, for they have been deceived by those spiritual forces of wickedness; they didn't know what they were really doing. Democracy, monarchy, fascism, communism and capitalism are all essentially based on the world order of Satan, whom the Bible calls the 'god of this world.' These systems will all fail because they are based upon the pride of man. Take, for instance, fascism and communism. They have a great deal in common. Both favor a personal dictatorship, a totalitarian form of government, a regimented citizenry and the sacrifice of individual welfare for the alleged common good. There is a major difference between them, however. While the fascists want to exterminate certain so-called inferior racial or religious groups in order to make room for the "superior" people like themselves, the communists, on the other hand, want to liquidate what they call enemies of the people — landlords, capitalists, etc. — in order to create what they call "utopia." Since it is much easier to change one's socio-economic status than to camouflage one's race or religion, the communists have an appeal unmatched by the fascists. They hate each other with great intensity, not because they are vastly different in ideology, but because, suprisingly enough, they both want to occupy the same place in the ideological circle. Thus, when we examine all these systems, they fail because the people who are in control are weak and soon fall prey to the dragon's wiles. Jesus does not promise us "utopia" down here, but He does promise that, if we will let Him come into our hearts, He will give us joy and peace by reigning in our hearts now, and, when He returns to earth, He will set up His Kingdom on earth as it is in Heaven.

Perhaps the two best ways we can help China now are: first, stand with the Chinese Christians in spiritual warfare and

How can we Help the Chinese Church Today?

Perhaps the two best ways we can help China now are: first, stand with the Chinese Christians in spiritual warfare and intercession to bind Satan's power over that land and loose the mighty power of the Holy Spirit with signs following, second, to go to China as teachers or technicians or in other professions, through an exchange program. China is asking help from the west in order to modernize their land, so they can feed their own people, educate them, house them and defend them. By doing this we are not condoning their governmental system, but are helping a great people who have suffered enough.

After all is said and done, it is the Chinese church that will evangelize China. The church planted with tears and watered with the blood of the martyrs. The church, not of the comfortable pew, but the church of the Cross: sending forth beautiful yellow feet on the mountains of China proclaiming the gospel of Peace. Let us stand with them in intercession and support them as the Lord opens doors of opportunity. "Our God reigns!"

After the testing is over and God begins to develop this vast universe that man has not even begun to explore, people of all nations, who have overcome Satan by the Blood of the Lamb, will reign with Him and work in close partnership with Him in this great universe. "To him that overcometh will I grant to sit with me in my throne" (Revelation 3:21 KJV).

We are optimistic because we have read the last chapter of the Bible. We know that the Cross will triumph over the Dragon. Let us be sure that we are "under the banner of the cross."

Chapter VIII

An Update On Tibet

I have just come back from a trip to the heart of Tibet (Lhasa – May 1984). The prayers and labours of faithful pioneers such as Ivan and Frances Kauffman are at last bearing fruit. High on a rocky crag overlooking the city of Lhasa (long the strong-hold of the most debased form of Buddhism) stands a large white cross. God has used the upheaval of the Communist take-over in China to open this forbidden land and break the power of the so called god-kings.

The Tibetan Bible was received with thankfullness even in the few remaining Lamasaries that we visited there. Some of the Tibetans that fled into exile in 1959 with the Dalai Lama have become Christians and we have reason to believe that seeds of the church that have been planted in Tibetan territory by Ivan and Frances Kauffman and others are bringing forth fruit. One of the last strong-holds of Satan has been invaded successfully. Only when the gospel of the kingdom is preached in all nations (ethnos) or people groups, will Jesus return to earth again. (Matt. 24:14).

The government of China is giving more liberty to the minority groups such as the Tibetans to practice their religions and the Monastaries are being restored. Pray that Satan's power to blind their eyes will continue to be broken and that both Tibetan and Chinese Christians may be thrust forth into this whitened harvest field.

Just as China built the Great Wall to keep out invaders from the North, so Satan has built a wall of darkness around this mountain kingdom to isolate it from the Gospel. But, praise God, Jesus said "I will build my church and the gates (and walls) of hell shall not prevail against it.".

Fervent prayer for Tibet has been very effective. Much has happened since the communists took over China, including the so called Tibet Autonomous Region and Chinghai (Quinghai), where the Tibetans have traditionally carried on their nomadic existence.

Of the over 2,400 lamaseries in Tibet, only 9 were left undamaged. The Dreprung Monastery, the largest in the world with over 10,000 lamas has been reduced to under 300, the rest being forced out into secular labour. In 1959 the Dalai Lama fled to North India after an abortive rebellion against Chinese rule. There they started schools for their children. The Tibetans felt they should learn English and invited Westerners to come and teach them. The Lord saw to it that the Westerners were Christian Missionaries. Today there are some 12 Tibetan Churches in that area with about as many Tibetan Pastors. God be praised. Christians in Nepal report a goodly number of Tibetans have followed the Lord Jesus Christ in that country just north of India.

The Chinese communists sent many Christians and pastors to Tibet to work in labour camps as a punishment for their so called religious activities. There they were forced to hard labour building roads over those high mountain passes etc. The enemy meant it for evil, but God meant it for good and through it brought the gospel into the heart of this strong-hold of Satan.

As some of our group climbed up the rocky crag to get a better look at the large white cross, they found it had been anchored into the rock by rivets fastened to the cross by a tripod-like support to withstand the high winds and storms of the roof of the world. Some Christian metalworker, exiled to Tibet, raised it as a signal of triumph of the cross over the dragon. We are not yet sure of the number of Tibetan Christians actually in Tibet itself, but at least the gates of hell have been broken down and the light of the gospel is shining where only darkness and fear reigned for so many centuries..

We saw pilgrims measuring their body lengths, prostrating themselves all the way to the temples to worship the idols. By this they hoped to gain favour with the spirits behind the idols, so that in their next rebirth they would not have it so hard. All they could look forward to is an endless vicious circle of rebirths, no peace. Our hearts were broken and we longed to lift them up and tell them of one who died and rose victorious to make a way for their rebirth into God's eternal kingdom of love. But alas they spoke only Tibetan. If our hearts were broken, what about the great heart of God who had sent His dear Son to shed His blood for their salvation?

We travelled over a 17,225 ft. pass to Shikaze, the second largest city in Tibet. There we visited Tashilumbo, the largest operating lamasery in Tibet with 600 lamas, the youngest being 11 years of age. These lamas are some of the few people that can read Tibetan, so we were especially anxious to put the Tibetan Bibles into their hands. The complete Tibetan Bible in its entirety had its first printing only in 1948. For over a half century Satan has hindered its completion. The manuscript of the entire Bible translated into the Tibetan language, which is much like ancient Sanskrit, was lost twice, and they had to begin again. What an example of what importance Satan gives to the written Word of God! He truly fears it.

When we saw with what readiness the lamas received the copies of the Word of God, we knew that there had been a victory in the heavenlies in answer to the prayers of God's people. Satan who had blinded and bound them for so many centuries no longer was able to do so.

It is to these pioneers of the cross who laboured on the borders of Tibet and at times ventured into that forbidden land at great cost that we dedicate this book. Ordinary men with a mighty Lord who gave them extraordinary Faith. "These all died in faith, not having received the promises, but having seen them afar off, and were persuaded of them, and embraced them, and confessed that they were strangers and pilgrims on the earth . . . of whom the world was not worthy." Hebrews 11:13, 38.

What has happened in China and Tibet is a testimony of the triumph of the Cross of love over the Dragon of fear. May we **who** follow be challenged to take up that Cross anew and follow in their train.

SPELLING LIST OF CHINESE NAMES AND PLACES

Modern Spelling for Chinese Names and Places
Used in this Book

PLACES

		NAMES	
Amoy	Xiamen	Pastor Chang	Pastor Zhang
Canton	Guangzhou	Chang Tso-lin	Zhang Zuo-lin
Chefoo	Yantai	Chang Ch'un-chiao	Zhang Chun-jiao
Choni	Jone	Chiang Ch'ing	Jiang Qing
Chungking	Chongqing	Elder Chin	Elder Jin
Foochow	Fuzhou	Chiang Kai-shek	Jiang Jai-shi
Grand Canal	Dayun He	Ch'ien Lung	Qian Long
Hankow	Hankou	Ch'ing Dynasty	Qing Dynasty
Kansu	Gansu	Chou En-lai	Zhou En-lai
Kiaochou Bay	Jiaozhou Wan	Elder Chou	Elder Zhou
Lanchow	Lanzhou	Feng Yu-Hsiang	Feng Yu-xiang
Nanking	Nanjing	Ho Chi-minh	He Qi-min
Ningpo	Ningbo	Pastor Hsia	Pastor Xia
Pearl River	Xi Jiang	Jung Kuo	Zhong Guo
Peking	Beijing	K'ang Hsi	Kang Xi
Shangtung	Shandong	Kwang Hsu	Kuang Xu
Shensi	Shanxi	Li Ta-chao	Li Da-zhao
Sian	Xi'an	Liu Shao-chi	Liu Shao-qi
Sinkiang	Xinjiang	Kuo Ming-tang	Guo Ming-dong
Swatow	Shantou	Mao-Tse-tung	Mao Ze-dong
Taochow	Taojo	Sheung Di	Shang Di
Tibet	Xizang	Soong Ch'ing-ling	Soong Qing-ling
Tientsin	Tianjin	Dr. Sun Yat-sen	Dr. Sun Yi-xian
Tsingtao	Qingdao	Sung Dynasty	Song Dynasty
Yangtze River	Chang Jiang	T'ang Dynasty	Tang Dynasty
Yellow River	Huang He	Teng Hsiao-ping	Wang Hung-zhen
Yellow Sea	Huang Hai	Wong Hung-jen	Deng Xiao-ping

FOOTNOTES

[1]Dick Wilson, **Asia Awakes** (London: Weidenfeld and Nicolson, 1970), p. 194.

[1a]Ibid., p. 193.

[2]Ibid., p. 194.

[3]Classics from Li Chi, **Book of Rites.**

[4]John C. Pollock, **A Foreign Devil in China** (Minneapolis, Minnesota: World-Wide Publications, 1971), p. 146.

[5]Mary A. Nourse, **A Short History of the Chinese** (New York: The Bobbs-Merrill Co., 1942), pp. 199-200.

[6]Frank M. Boyd, **God's Wonderful Book** (Springfield: Gospel Publishing House, 1933), p. 122.

[7]Ibid., p. 122.

[8]William H. Hudspeth, **The Bible & China,** p. 12.

[9]Jean Chesneaux, Francoise Le Babrier, and Marie-Claire Bergere, **China from the Opium War to the 1911 Revolution** (New York: Pantheon Books, 1977).

[10]Frank Edmond, "Report on the Death of Ivan Kauffman," **The Pentecostal Testimony** (Toronto: Full Gospel Publishing House), May 1934, p. 10.

[11]A. G. Ward, "Report on the Death of Ivan Kauffman," **The Pentecostal Testimony** (Toronto: Full Gospel Publishing House), May 1934, p. 10.

[12]**The Guinness Book of Records 1980** (New York: Sterling Publishing Co., Inc., 1980), p. 190.

[13]Jonathon Goforth, **By My Spirit** (Minneapolis, Minnesota: Bethany Fellowship, 1964), pp. 14-15.

[14]Ibid., p. 17.

[15]Ivan Kauffman, "Report from North China," **The Pentecostal Testimony** (Toronto: Full Gospel Publishing House), May 1931, p. 9.

[16]"Report from North China," **The Pentecostal Testimony** (Toronto: Full Gospel Publishing House), August 1931, p. 14.

[17]John C. Pollock, **A Foreign Devil in China** (Minneapolis, Minnesota: World-Wide Publications, 1971), p. 246.

[18]Personal notes on Chou En-lai.

[19]Rev. Clare Scratch, **The Shangtung Revival.**

BIBLIOGRAPHY

Boyd, Frank M. **God's Wonderful Book**. Springfield: Gospel Publishing House,1933.

Chao, Jonathan. **History of Christianity in China**. Pamphlet, 1978.

Chesneaux, Jean; Le Babrier, Francoise; and Bergere, Marie-Claire. **China from the Opium War to the 1911 Revolution**. New York: Pantheon Books, 1977.

Gascoyne-Cecil, Lord William. **Changing China**. London: James Nisbet & Co. Ltd., 1911.

Goforth, Jonathan. **By My Spirit**. Minneapolis, Minnesota: Bethany Fellowship, 1964.

Hudspeth, William H. **The Bible & China**.

Leys, Simon. **Chinese Shadows**. New York: The Viking Press, 1977.

Li, Dun J., Ph. D. **The Ageless Chinese — A History**. New York: Charles Scribner's Sons, 1978.

McAleavry, Henry. **Modern History of China**. New York: Weidenfeld & Nicholson, 1967.

Mosley, George. **China Since 1911**. New York: Harper, 1968.

China, Empire to People's Republic. London: B. T. Batsford Ltd., 1968.

Nourse, Mary A. **A Short History of the Chinese**. New York: The Bobbs-Merrill Co.,, 1942.

Pollock, John C. **A Foreign Devil in China**. Minneapolis, Minnesota: World-Wide Publications, 1971.

Potter, Charles Francis. **The Great Religious Leaders**. New York: Simon and Schuster, Inc., 1962.

Pye, Lucian W. **China, An Introduction**. Boston: Little, Brown & Co., 1972.

Wilson, Dick. **Asia Awakes**. London: Weidenfeld & Nicolson, 1970.

Wylie, Roy. **China, An Introduction for Canadians**. Toronto: Peter Martin Assoc. Ltd., 1973.

Yang, Y. C. **China's Religious Heritage**. New York: Abingdon-Cokesbury Press, 1943.

Personal notes on Chou En-lai.

Book of Rites. Classics from Li Chi.

The Guinness Book of Records 1980. New York: Sterling Publishing Co. Inc., 1980.

Kauffman, Ivan. "Report from North China," **The Pentecostal Testimony,** (August 1931). Toronto: Full Gospel Publishing House.

Edmond, Frank; and Ward, A. G. "Report on the Death of Ivan Kauffman," **The Pentecostal Testimony,** (May 1934). Toronto: Full Gospel Publishing House.